D0875275

sugar

Micheal Ray Richardson,
Eighties Excess, and the NBA

CHARLEY ROSEN

University of Nebraska Press | Lincoln and London

Library of Congress Cataloging-in-Publication Data
Names: Rosen, Charles, author.
Title: Sugar: Micheal Ray Richardson,
 eighties excess, and the NBA / Charley Rosen.
Description: Lincoln: University of Nebraska Press, 2018.
Identifiers: LCCN 2017038778
ISBN 9781496202161 (hardback: alk. paper)
ISBN 9781496206121 (epub)
ISBN 9781496206138 (mobi)
ISBN 9781496206145 (pdf)
Subjects: LCSH: Richardson, Micheal Ray. |
Basketball players—United States—Biography. |
Basketball—United States—History. | National
Basketball Association—History. | BISAC: SPORTS
& RECREATION / Basketball.
Classification: LCC GV884.R523 R67 2018 |
DDC 796.323092 [B]—dc23
LC record available at https://lccn.loc.gov/2017038778

Set in Minion Pro by Mikala R Kolander.

Contents

Preface

Not even Micheal Ray Richardson blames his fall from the so-called Nigger Heaven on anything or anybody but himself. And his fall was as personally devastating as was Lucifer's decent into hell. But unlike Lucifer, and although he too suffered greatly, Micheal Ray was eventually able to redeem himself.

Indeed, Richardson's long, torturous climb from the depths of his personal agony into becoming a respectable and useful member of society is as inspiring as his fall was shameful and degrading.

So, then, Micheal Ray Richardson's story from top to bottom and back to the top is nothing less than inspirational to all of us mortals who have sinned against others and, most importantly, sinned against ourselves.

Prologue *December 27, 1985—Moonachie, New Jersey*

There were several reasons why the mood at the New Jersey Nets' annual post-Christmas party was unabashedly celebratory. After all, weren't the Nets riding high with a record of 23-14? Wasn't their roster loaded with such potent young talent as Mike Gminski, Buck Williams, Darryl Dawkins, Albert King, and especially the dazzling Micheal Ray Richardson? And hadn't they demonstrated their kinetic potential just eighteen months ago when they had upset the defending champion Philadelphia 76ers in the first round of the playoffs? No wonder the owner of the team, Joe Taub, was brimming with optimism.

"Jersey Joe" was born in Paterson, where his father, an immigrant from Poland, eked out enough money to support the family by driving a horse-drawn cart though the streets of the city buying and selling junk.

Taub played basketball at Eastside High School and became a devotee of the sport. He developed another lifelong passion while a student at Temple University—an interest in entrepreneurial promotions. That's where he and a fellow classmate, Bill Cosby, booked acts for a school show titled *The Hour of Pleasure*. One act booked for $50.00 by Taub and Cosby was a virtually unknown folk-rock group called the Mamas and the Papas. The band was paid $35.00 and Taub and Cosby each earned $7.50. Numbers meant money, so after graduating from Temple, Taub found employment as an accountant.

At age twenty-one, Joe and his older brother Henry founded a business that soon became Automatic Data Processing, a firm that printed checks for large industries. By 1985 Taub's company employed a work force of thirty thousand and grossed $3.5 billion annually. In addition to his many local philanthropic avocations, Taub had headed a syndicate that purchased the Long Island–based Nets in 1978 and moved them to Piscataway, New Jersey.

He was a short, trim septuagenarian who, in his tailored pin-striped, double-breasted suits, with his sharp grey eyes, and his heart-shaped head topped by a coiffed helmet of thick gray hair, could easily pass for a fifty-year-old still lingering in the prime of life.

And if Taub saw himself as father figure and patron to all of his players, he had a special fondness for Richardson. That's because, since Richardson had already failed two official drug tests, the exuberantly immature Richardson needed more supportive attention than the rest. And Taub wholeheartedly believed his best player's vows that he had quit drugs and would stay clean forever more. After all, who was two-faced enough to lie to Jersey Joe?

And, hey, 'twas the season to be jolly.

So Taub had gone to considerable expense to make sure that all of the Nets employees would have a bang-up time in a private, windowless, mirror-walled room in George's Restaurant in Moonachie, New Jersey, just a short drive from the Nets' practice court. Indeed, he'd sprung for $7,000 for the top-of-the-line "Grand Buffet"—featuring everything from filet mignon to seafood paella, from chicken piccata to baked Virginia ham. All available at carving stations or served from real silver chafing dishes. There was also an open bar and waiters in tuxedos circulating through the one hundred or so guests bearing trays of bite-sized shrimp and chicken goodies. A "hip" DJ cost Taub another $250.

Dozens of tables were arranged around the fringes of the dance floor, each table covered with a white linen tablecloth that matched the napkins, also with fancy translucent china, crystal glassware, gleaming utensils, flowers, candles, the works. However, very few of those on hand bothered to sit at the tables, preferring instead to dance on the brown-and-tan marbleized floor as the DJ played the hits of the day: Springsteen, Michael Jackson, Van Halen, and even the Talking Heads. As a concession to "the brothers," the room also rocked with disco tunes, and Kool & the Gang was still cool enough.

By far the happiest of the Nets players was Micheal "Sugar" Ray Richardson, and his joy was understandable: At age thirty, he was in the second season of a four-year $3 million contract. His wife had just given birth to a baby boy, and Richardson had rewarded her with a brand-new, silver-hued Mercedes-Benz convertible. (His was gold colored.) Even better he was already a four-time All-Star and was playing like a guaranteed future Hall of Famer. Only a few weeks ago, Larry Bird had said this about Sugar Ray: "He's the best basketball player on the planet."

For sure, Micheal's not-so-distant past was a haze of habitual drug and alcohol abuse. He had previously tested positive twice for cocaine and on several occasions had been forced to spend time in rehab centers. But he was convinced that he had learned his lesson, that he was "cured." And hadn't he been certified clean for just over two years? The NBA had even recruited Richardson to appear in *Cocaine Drain*, a widely disseminated antidrug video. "Cleaner than Mister Clean," he says of that time. "And playing the best basketball of my career."

Besides, at the behest of Taub, Richardson's best buddy and teammate was on hand to look out for him. That would be Darryl

Dawkins, aka Chocolate Thunder, all six feet eleven, 270 pounds of him—famous for tearing down rims and joyfully claiming he was from the planet Lovetron. However, even though he'd been in the NBA for eight years, Dawkins remained a man-child and underachieving player. Off the court, Dawkins was the team jester and party-time ring leader. Always ready for a good time, he devoured the bountiful feast of his life with two hungry hands. Most importantly, Big Double-D was no stranger to illicit drug use; had seen, heard, and used everything; and always knew what was what.

So there was Sugar Ray, his round face split with a wide, sparkling smile that bent his thin moustache into a shallow U-shape, while his high cheekbones and thick black brows squeezed his flashing brown eyes. Festive in his fashionable light-blue casual suit, Richardson was dancing with this guy's secretary, that guy's assistant, the other guy's bookkeeper.

C'mon, ladies. Spin the light fantastic with the Sugar Man. He'll make you feel happy, important, beautiful.

When the DJ took a short break, Richardson wandered over to the bar where Dawkins was inhaling a bottle of beer. The two pals were quickly joined by Bobby Cattage, a big-chested six-foot-seven rookie from a small town in Louisiana, a stranger in paradise who yearned to be as "with it" as Dawkins and Richardson.

Dawkins took to informing the rook about what a jerk Isiah Thomas was: "If you're driving down the lane and he's right there? The little shit'll step on your plant foot, something the three blind mice never see, something that can fuck up your knee and end your career in a hurry. So when you get a chance to foul the fucker, lay the wood to him. No matter how hard you hit him they can only give you one foul."

"Y-y-y-yeah," said Richardson. "M-m-make him p-pick his b-b-black ass off the f-floor and hit two f-f-free throws."

The rookie nodded in eager agreement. He couldn't wait to earn his bona fides and fuck up Thomas.

Their small conference was interrupted when a young woman rushed past them, a newly hired secretary to one of Taub's legion of lawyers. She was a somewhat thin redhead, overdressed in a blue chiffon cocktail dress. Dawkins took a quick look and pronounced her to be "unfuckable."

The players watched as she approached her boss, a gray-haired man stuffed into a fat brown suit. They were both a little tipsy and spoke loud enough for the three players to overhear.

It seems she was unfamiliar with exactly where she was and worried about the heavy snow that had begun to fall. She needed directions to her apartment in Irvington and was offered two choices. A circuitous journey via various parkways and highways, or a short-cut through East Orange that would save fifteen minutes.

She opted for the latter route, "before the snow gets really bad."

The lawyer said to take a right here, a left there, veer this way around the park, and so on. But he warned her that East Orange was a dangerous neighborhood. "Make sure to lock your car door," he said. "And if you're stopped at a red light and somebody approaches you, then just go through the light. . . . The night belongs to them."

Dawkins snorted and said to his teammates, "Let's get the fuck out of here."

The rookie was quick to second the motion. "Where to?" he asked.

"The Sports Bar at the Sheraton," Dawkins said. Then he turned to face Richardson. "You coming, Sugar?"

"N-n-nah. I'm g-going straight home." His wife, the baby. Besides, his sister had just flown in from Denver to spend the rest of the holiday with them.

Micheal can never forget what happened next: "It was snow-ing like we were at the North Pole, so I was in kind of a hurry to get home. But, on the way there, I had to pass the hotel anyway, so I thought, what the hell, I'd just stop by for a few minutes. It was one of the worst decisions I ever made."

The Sports Bar in nearby Aspen Heights had the obligatory mirror-backed bar, several wall- and pillar-mounted TV sets tuned to various sporting events: games of soccer, basketball, tennis, and hockey. A space large enough for dancing separated the bar from a small dining room. Above all, the Sports Bar was always swarming with friendly young women.

"It was a real hot spot," says Micheal. "A lot of the guys would go there after games, and it was also a favorite after-practice des-tination for the New York Giants. So the single, on-the-make women knew where the rich athletes would be. Normally, though, I stayed away from there."

Once he entered the Sports Bar that fateful evening, however, Micheal lingered to dance, sign some autographs, and slug down several generous shots of bourbon. "That was the start of it all," he says. "I was feeling good. Real good."

Meanwhile, Dawkins had other plans. He had a date with a beautiful light-skinned girl to do some hot-and-heavy mattress bouncing over at his house. Besides, Sugar was drinking and laughing and having fun. Dawkins knew that Richardson wasn't supposed to be drinking, but he seemed to be totally under con-trol. So Dawkins went over to Cattage, told the rook that he had to go, and asked if he could keep tabs on Sugar. And Cattage said, "No problem."

After a few more drinks, a good-looking blonde approached Richardson. He'd seen her there once or twice, but they'd never spoken to each other, not even to say hello. Anyway, she was coming on to him now real strong. Dispensing with the prelimi-naries, she said she'd fuck him like he'd never been fucked before.

White chicks, black chicks, yellow chicks, even a red one once in Houston, he'd had them all. As far as Sugar was concerned a pussy was a pussy. Still, he was haunted by the memory of his childhood in Lubbock, a dusty, nowhere shit hole in the Texas Panhandle. Where the crackers mercilessly made fun of his stuttering. They laughed whenever he dared to speak in school— not that the teachers ever called on him. And the white bitches were even more abusive than the guys, calling him "M-m-mumumbles." It wasn't so bad when his mom moved the family to Denver, but only when he became the star of the high-school team in his senior year.

Yeah, so he took a certain relish in fucking white chicks. Besides, unlike many of the greedy hellcat sisters he'd been with, no white chick ever called him "nigger."

Richardson was also well aware that his postpartum wife was in a special state, super-sensitive, not wanting to make love or even to be touched. Monogamy was not his thing anyway, and he was more than a little horny. Besides, the blonde was eminently fuckable. "Okay, let's g-go d-d-do it."

And Bobby Cattage?

"I turned away from Sugar for about a minute, right? And when I turned back around, he was gone. I ran outside just in time to see him drive off with some white girl in a gold-colored Mercedes. It was snowing like crazy, but he had the top down. And nobody saw him for another three or four days."

"She was a businesswoman," says Richardson. "She was attracted to me and was just out for a good time. I never did find out what her name was, and I can't even remember exactly what she looked like."

They drove to her apartment—"a nice, classy place." Then she pulled a bag of goodies out of a drawer in the bedroom. Coke to snort. Coke to smoke. Richardson figured he could handle one dose. "But I was wrong."

The first round landed Richardson in sex heaven. "We were banging away and howling with pleasure. But the second dose wasn't as good as the first, and every hit from then on had less and less effect. Still, a druggie winds up chasing a ghost. Doing it just to do it. And we were still heavy into our fuckathon."

If the coke made Richardson more alert to the moment, it also obliterated his overall sense of time's passing. "The only things that mattered were the drugs, the sex, and the paranoia. The fucking paranoia got worse and worse, because I knew I shouldn't be doing what I was doing. But, man, I was so motherfucking high, so wrapped up in the drugs."

Meanwhile, the TV was always on, never off. "But it was just background stuff that we didn't pay attention to. Looking without seeing, hearing without listening. But then, on the third day, I couldn't help noticing my own picture on the screen and a voiceover saying that Micheal Ray Richardson was missing. They said it was feared that I'd been kidnapped and might even be dead. "So I shouted at the TV, 'Hey, motherfucker, I ain't missing. I'm right here!'"

Oh, shit. That's when Richardson came back into real time. He had missed two practice sessions and one ball game. Desperate to cover himself, he called the Nets and said he'd just escaped from kidnappers. Then he went home.

If Richardson suddenly realized where he was and where he was supposed to be, for several years David Stern had a similar awareness regarding the state of the NBA. The league was currently in trouble on many levels, and despite featuring razzle-dazzle action and the world's greatest athletes, the popular appeal of NBA action was noticeably diminishing.

If game attendance for the current regular season was actually up a tick from the 1984–85 campaign (to an average of 11,893), the slight increase (257 fans per game) was primarily due to the presence of three heralded rookies—Hakeem Olajuwon, Charles Barkley, and Michael Jordan. Even so, only the account ledgers of New York, Chicago, and the Los Angeles Lakers were recorded in black ink.

More ominous was the decrease in the previous season's play-off attendance—14,391, down from a peak of 17,048 in 1979. This particular situation verged on catastrophe since NBA teams looked to these "extra" games as providing a huge income bonanza.

And what would happen when the deeds of Olajuwon, Barkley, and Jordan became routine? Who was foolish enough to believe that any or all of these young black players would have sufficient charisma to overcome the institutional racism that plagued virtually every facet of American culture?

Just ten short years before in the 1974–75 season, black players composed only 71 percent of those NBA players who had logged one thousand or more total minutes. In 1985 that total was up to 81 percent. However, because the city of Boston had a long tradition of antiblack fervor—more than once, Bill Russell's house there was broken into and the intruders defecated on his bed—the Celtics roster featured six white players: Larry Bird, Kevin McHale, Danny Ainge, Scott Wedman, Bill Walton, and Jerry Sichting. Discounting the Celtics, then, the presence of minute-intensive blacks in the NBA rose to 83.2 percent.

Worse still, the secret corps of detectives hired by the NBA had discovered that one of the league's superstars was snorting heroin. Also that several dozen high-profile white players were habitually tooting and/or smoking coke.

This information was kept under cover lest the integrity of the game be destroyed, many of the league's marquee players revealed as over-the-top druggies, and the NBA wind up being reduced to a minor blip in Sports America.

Moreover, there were widespread public rumors concerning a drug ring that centered on most of the Phoenix Suns players.

A convicted drug dealer testified that he had made "at least thirty" drug sales to Neal Walk, the Suns high-scoring center. Plus, Johnny High, one of the Suns' best players, had recently been shot and killed in mysterious circumstances. Players in the know around the league understood that this had been a gangland slaying that was directly connected with the Suns' involvement in the drug trade.

Also, the NBA was negotiating with the Turner Broadcasting System to continue telecasting regular-season games. The 1985–86 season would conclude their $20 million two-year deal—which, subtracting the monies directed to the league office, left each franchise with about $700,000. Useful income, to be sure, but not enough to guarantee an overall profit. And because of the high volume of black players and the drug-related deaths that had the media calling the NBA "an outlaw league," plus the fact that vast majority of fans who could afford cable TV were white, the negotiations were difficult.

Something had to be done not only to discourage drug use, but also to whiten-up the league. No wonder NBA commissioner David Stern was frantic.

One of Stern's attempted solutions would involve Micheal Ray Richardson. However, more significantly, the issues concurrent with the unfolding of Sugar Ray's life mirror what was (and still is) wrong with not only the NBA but also with many aspects of American culture.

To wit: racism, anti-Semitism, selective justice, drug abuse, sexism, macho-bred immaturity, the lack of personal responsibility for misdeeds, and the mindless adoration of celebrities.

Living on Dreams

Richardson was born in Lubbock, Texas, on April 11, 1955. "My father was Billy Jack Richardson," says Micheal Ray, "and since he was in the army, throughout those early days he would come and go. When I was six, he was gone for good. That's when Luddie, my mom, decided to get us all out of Lubbock—a nowhere place that was all dirt roads and hot as hell." The family (two older brothers and three younger sisters) wound up in Denver. "'To get us a better life,' she told us."

Micheal says he was Luddie's favorite, and that she was "the sweetheart" of his life. "'I'm the mother and the daddy, too,' she used to say, and she was. She worked in the kitchen at Colorado General Hospital and was on her feet all day. When she came home I'd rub skin lotion into her sore feet. 'Don't worry, Momma,' I'd tell her. 'Someday I'm gonna have lots of money. I'll buy you a house and then your feet won't hurt anymore.'"

Richardson never blamed anybody for his subsequent misdeeds. "When you willfully do something," he has said, "no matter what it is, you have to take full responsibility. That's why, even with all I've been through, I've always taken 100 percent of the responsibility." Even so, there were several unfortunate circumstances of his childhood that greatly influenced the negative decisions Richardson made as an adult.

There's an enormous body of literature proving that African American boys raised by single mothers have difficult lives ahead of them. Indeed, 72 percent of black males in America are raised by single mothers—as opposed to 25.8 percent of the total population. Furthermore, studies show that single mothers are much stricter with their daughters than they are with their sons. The boys are routinely coddled, and their poor behavior easily excused. As a result, these youngsters are at a higher risk of engaging in drug and alcohol abuse, of being less cooperative with authority figures, having damaging emotional problems, and possessing a weaker sense of right and wrong. Moreover, they have poor impulse control and are incapable of delaying gratification, which usually leads to sexual promiscuity.

The youngsters generally feel betrayed and insulted by their departed father and see themselves as victims of universal injustice. This leads to self-hatred and an inability to deal with either failure or success. Still another result is the development of "father hunger," that is, the desperate search for a male adult to take the place of the missing father.

In a sense, Richardson got off easy only because 72 percent of adolescent murderers are mother-raised black males, as are 43 percent of the national prison population and 60 percent of convicted rapists. Otherwise, Richardson's adult years neatly, and tragically, fit many aspects of this unfortunate scenario. It should be noted, however, that most of these traits were not manifest until he began abusing drugs.

"I also grew up with a serious speech impediment," says Richardson, "a pronounced lisp and stutter. Sometimes it was impossible for anybody to understand what I was trying to say. Because we moved into a black and Spanish section of Denver, the white kids had another reason to tease me and sometimes beat me up. I tried getting back at them by laughing at this guy's big nose, or that guy's bad skin. But what I was supposed to do was shuffle around and act like a darkie, so my making fun of them only brought more abuse my way."

It used to be that a child's stuttering was believed to be caused by an overprotective parent, usually the mother. This view was abandoned in favor of the cause being a matter of a child's language and thought development progressing quicker than the motor abilities for producing speech. While 10 percent of preschool children stutter, 90 percent stop by the age of twelve. However, Richardson would become one of the 1 percent of adult stutterers.

Ross Barrett of the Center for Stuttering says that stuttering is four times more common in young boys than in young girls. "The current research," says Barrett, "also shows that there is no emotional cause for stuttering. In fact, stuttering is a genetically disposed condition that can be located in the twelfth chromosome. However, we don't know why 1 percent of child stutterers continue stuttering as adults. It probably has something to do with brain chemistry."

In any event, Richardson is merely the latest in a long line of adult stutterers: Demosthenes famously put pebbles in his mouth in an attempt to cure himself. Others include Aristotle, George Washington, Thomas Jefferson, Isaac Newton, Charles Darwin, Theodore Roosevelt, Lenin, and Louis the Stammerer, who was the king of France in 877–79.

In any case, while Richardson's stutter initially limited his opportunities to express himself outside the basketball court, once he became a star he lost all his inhibitions and was unafraid to say whatever he thought in any company and in any circumstances.

The first of Richardson's many father figures was Donald Wilson, the principal of his elementary school. "He was the one who encouraged me and helped me to discover that playing basketball was the only way I could truly express myself."

Richardson moved on to all-black Manuel High School and made the varsity as a freshman. "I didn't play much at first, but while most of the kids were running around, smoking reefer, and drinking Mad Dog 20-20, which was the cheapest wine they could get their hands on, I was a good kid and totally focused on basketball." He would even shovel the snow covering a nearby playground basketball court so he could practice his shooting. And he used to dream about playing in the National Basketball Association (NBA): "One night I had to wake up everybody to tell them that I'd just dreamt that I dunked over Julius Erving."

Richardson blossomed in his senior year, and he had an outstanding state tournament, leading his team to the championship game where they lost to an all-white team. "All of a sudden," he says, "I was a hero and the same people who tortured me now wanted to kiss my ass." He even had his choice of girls who were also begging for his attention.

Richardson then accepted a scholarship offer from the University of Montana: "The only one I received." But in truth, it was Micheal Ray himself who initiated the contact.

George Melvin "Jud" Heathcote was Montana's coach, and his recruiting efforts were focused on the point guard on the team that beat Manuel High School to win the state championship. "But," said Heathcote, "the kid had a lot of family problems so he decided to go to a school that was closer to home." As a result, Heathcote was "scrambling" for a guard.

"Out of nowhere," Heathcote said, "I got a phone call from a guy who says, 'Hi, I'm Micheal Ray Richardson.' He told me that he knew the guard I wanted had gone elsewhere, that he was a friend of so-and-so, and he heard that Missoula was a nice place, so he'd like to come up there. So I called my assistant coach, Jim Brandenburg, and asked who the hell Micheal Ray Richardson was. And he said, 'He's a six-three forward from Manuel High School in Denver.' And I said, 'I'm not looking for any six-three forwards.' Brandenburg says, 'Well, maybe he can play guard, I don't know.'"

Because Heathcote's hoops program was chronically underfunded, he was always looking to catch lightning in a bottle. Without making any commitment, Heathcote then invited Richardson to come to Missoula for a visit.

Under the existing NCAA rules, coaches were prohibited from either working out potential recruits or even watching them scrimmage on campus. But Heathcote and Brandenburg stationed themselves near a doorway and snuck a few quick peeks as Richardson played pickup games with some of the holdover varsity players. "My God," said Heathcote to his assistant. "Has he got some quick hands! Let's give him a scholarship."

If Heathcote stretched the rules a wee bit, many of his contemporaries were secretly tearing them to shreds. For example, while no-show jobs and money under the table were common inducements powerhouse programs employed to attract blue-chip recruits, a certain southwestern college routinely sent an assistant coach on recruiting trips with a suitcase filled with at least $20,000 in cash. Even worse, this particular assistant—who had played in the NBA and eventually returned to the league as an assistant—habitually kept half the money for himself.

The primary function of another assistant at a southern school—also an NBA vet—was to make sure that recruits who visited the campus were provided with hookers.

Moreover, the standard recruiting ploy of an assistant at a midwestern college was to bed down the single mothers of the young men he was recruiting.

The list approaches infinity, but the most egregious violation concerned an East Coast college that provided a drug-addicted, yet much sought after, high-school player with heroin.

"Living in Missoula was a shock," Richardson recalls, "especially since I was the only black player on the team. But my momma had taught me to love people for what they were, so I learned to live with them and learned about who they were. My roommate was as country as a cow pie, and so were most of my new teammates. It took me about two months to make the adjustment. Keg parties were the big deal on campus, and that was fine with me. Otherwise I lived like a nerd. And I was so homesick that every other weekend I drove eighteen hundred miles roundtrip to visit my family."

During his freshman season, Richardson grew an outsized Afro and averaged 7.5 points per game. When a girl he was dating became pregnant, Richardson married her in the summer of 1975. The next year he boosted his average to 18.2 points per game, led the Montana Grizzlies to the school's first-ever Big Sky Conference championship, and into the National Collegiate Athletic Association (NCAA) tournament—where they reached the regional finals before losing a close game to John Wooden's mighty University of California, Los Angeles Bruins. In recognition of his outstanding play, Richardson was named to the all-conference first team.

"I was very close to Heathcote," says Richardson. "I came to him with all of my troubles, and he was very supportive and helpful in many ways. Anyway, after my sophomore season, Heathcote left to take over at Michigan State where he'd be working with Magic Johnson. I was devastated. 'Don't go!' I pleaded. 'You're like a father to me.' Then I started crying my eyes out. 'Coach, you can't leave me. I don't have a father.' But there was nothing I could do."

Richardson was so dependent on Heathcote that he wanted to transfer to Michigan. "No," said Heathcote. "Your place is here."

When Jim Brandenburg succeeded Heathcote, it didn't take long for Richardson and his new coach to develop a close relationship. "I was so hungry for a father figure," says Richardson, "that almost any man who smiled at me and was nice to me would do." Over the next two seasons, Richardson's scoring improved to a team-best 19.2 and then 24.2 points per game. In addition, he set the pace in rebounds and assists. Inspired by his own success and the celebrity of boxer "Sugar" Ray Robinson, Richardson also started referring to himself as "Sugar."

Brandenburg has nothing but praise for his star player: "Micheal was always a good kid, a good practice player and a hard worker. If we had featured him more, he could have scored thirty or forty points every game. We knew we couldn't do that because our opponents would triple-team him, and he'd be totally out of the mix."

The Grizzlies had a record of 20-9 in Richardson's last season at Montana, but an overtime loss to Weber State in the second round of the Big Sky tournament kept them out of the NCAA's Big Dance.

No surprise, though, when Richardson was selected to play in a senior all-star game in Hawaii. Leading up to this game, Micheal Ray was projected as being a low first- or high second-round draft pick. "But then I kicked everybody's ass," he says. "Reggie Theus, Phil Ford, Butch Lee—I made them all look like shit. Suddenly everybody was telling me that I would go top five in the upcoming NBA draft."

Away from his wife, his new-born daughter, and the provincial world of Missoula, Richardson took full advantage of his freedom.

Besides NBA coaches, general managers, and scouts, the scene was crawling with agents. "All of the agents used the same inducements; fixing us up with Hawaiian girls. Most of them were ugly bitches, but I was living in a fantasy world so I fucked all comers."

The 1978 NBA college draft was a low-key affair, closed to the public, and dependent upon wire services to report the results. Which were as follows:

1. Portland, Mychal Thompson from Minnesota
2. Kansas City, Phil Ford from North Carolina
3. Indiana, Rick Robey from Kentucky
4. New York, Micheal Ray Richardson, Montana

Most notably, Boston selected Larry Bird sixth, and Philadelphia picked Mo Cheeks in the second round (thirty-sixth overall). San Antonio based its first-round pick (Frankie Sanders from Southern University, twentieth overall) strictly on the information on the back of a Topps bubble gum card.

In any event, the Knicks were thrilled to have secured the rights to Richardson. Knicks coach, Willis Reed, heralded Richardson as the "next Walt Frazier."

2

Living the Dream

His first pro contract guaranteed $909,000 (worth $3.2 million today) for four years. And he immediately bought a Mercedes-Benz 450SL that featured the word "Sugar" embossed on the stick shift in large gold letters.

Richardson's meet-and-greet press conference in Madison Square Garden was a disaster. "The first question they asked me was why my nickname was 'Sugar.' Well, I was very nervous, and with my stuttering and all, it took me about three or four minutes to answer. 'Because my game's so sweet.' Man, those New York media guys were looking at me like I was a leper, and their reports just ripped me up, down, and sideways."

Once the season started it didn't take long for Richardson to realize, "I simply wasn't ready for the NBA."

In truth, college and pro ball are two vastly different versions of the same thing—like scrambled and hard-boiled eggs. The NBA is faster (up and down the court), quicker (speed in a limited area), and much more physical. Whereas college teams might have five or six different offensive sets, NBA ballclubs usually have anywhere from fifteen to twenty—and the same differential exists in defensive alignments and rotations. As a result, rookies have to make more decisions—and make them quicker—than they did in the college game.

It should be noted, however, that because the draft rules have changed over the years to enable players to turn pro after playing only one year in college, rookies are even more unprepared for the power, speed, and intricacies of NBA action. With so many young, raw players on NBA rosters, coaches have been forced to dumb down their game plans. That's one reason why we see so many high pick and rolls, which is essentially rather uncomplicated two-man basketball. And which is why today's rookies have an easier time adjusting and making an impact.

But in the 1978–79 season, Richardson was lost.

The NBA made little sense. Ray Williams was the Knicks' young, dynamic shooting guard whose ability to sky over big men was powered by his unusually large thighs. In fact Williams's thighs were too muscular to fit comfortably into the tight uniform shorts that NBA teams wore back then. "Girls' shorts!" Richardson huffed. "Hot pants!" In order to avoid the pinching and occasional cramping that resulted, Williams took a pair of scissors and reduced the pressure by cutting two- or three-inch slits on each side of the shorts. And the NBA fined him fifty dollars!

And whereas veteran players could cuss referees with impunity, a raised eyebrow was sufficient to get a rookie nailed with a technical foul. Moreover, established stars like Moses Malone, Bob McAdoo, Kareem Abdul-Jabbar, Artis Gilmore, Elvin Hayes, and Truck Robinson wouldn't get tooted for committing fouls unless the contact drew blood. But if a rookie so much as scratched his own ass . . . ?

Willis Reed was Richardson's latest coach-cum-father figure and he tried to help: "Willis took me under his wing. I was playing about twenty minutes a game, and I thought I was making slow, but steady progress. But I was still mostly confused."

Too bad Reed lacked the communication skills and the necessary basketball IQ to be an effective NBA head coach. As a player, he was all heart and grit, but when the "old" Knicks of the late '60s and early '70s would convene in a huddle, Red Holzman would often ask the likes of Bill Bradley, Phil Jackson, Jerry Lucas, Dave DeBusschere, and Walt Frazier, "What the hell is going on out there?" And whenever Reed volunteered an opinion, he was told by his teammates to "shut the fuck up."

Even so, Reed believed in Richardson and was always encouraging.

"The team wasn't doing so well," says Micheal Ray, "until we won five games on a tough six-game road trip to the West Coast. Don't you know that the team's owner, Sonny Werblin, met us when we landed in New York at midnight and fired Willis on the spot. Damn!"

In an effort to restore the Knicks' glory years, fifty-eight-year-old Red Holzman moved from his cushy consultant's role to the team's bench. "Sure," says Richardson, "Holzman had won two championships years before, but he was an older man and very set in his ways. Besides, Holzman didn't like rookies. Didn't like them and wouldn't play them.

"Jim Cleamons and Ray Williams were the starting guards, and me and my roommate Mike Glenn were the backups. What happened a lot was that the team would be getting their doors blown off so Holzman would put me and Mike into the game. We'd play lights out and get us right back into the game, then Holzman would reinsert the vets, and we'd go back to getting the shit kicked out of us. Needless to say, Holzman and I did not get along very well."

After being the Man at Montana, Richardson couldn't get used to being a mere sub. Also, Holzman added to his distress and confusion by sometimes playing him at guard and sometimes at small forward.

One morning, while Jud Heathcote and his Michigan Wolverines were in New York, Richardson and his former coach breakfasted together. Heathcote listened to Richardson's litany of woes and counseled patience. Richardson should never doubt his own talents and should just keep playing hard. Sooner or later cream always rises to the top.

If Heathcote's fatherly advice soothed Richardson, the rookie's game failed to improve. "I was still playing like a dud, so I didn't want to be seen in public. It was bad enough that the Knick fans at the Garden booed every time I stepped on to the court, but some of them even started throwing eggs at me. What the fuck? Man, that season I lived like a monk."

Except, that is, for exercising his primary release and satisfaction: driving his Mercedes-Benz wildly through the streets of New York at maximum speed. "You got to drive like this," he told Glenn, "or you won't get anywhere."

Confronted with what he believed to be a stubborn, uncaring authority figure, Richardson snapped. "Finally," he says, "I couldn't take it anymore, so on my own I called a press conference. My first announcement was that Holzman didn't know what the fuck he was doing. My second announcement was I wanted the Knicks to trade me and get me out of town as soon as possible. Naturally, that didn't help my situation at all. I mean, what did I know? I was a young kid who never had a father to teach me how to be a man. I was impulsive, pig headed, and didn't know what was right and what was wrong. Not only did I feel unloved, but I felt unlovable."

When the interminable, humiliating season finally ground to a stop, the Knicks' record was 31-51 (25-43 under Holzman), and Richardson's stats were equally as dismal: career lows in field-goal and free-throw percentages (.414 and .539), assists (3.0), rebounds (3.2), and most disappointing points per game (6.5).

In other words, except for the likes of Wilt Chamberlain, Bill Russell, Elgin Baylor, and Elvin Hayes, whose special talents enabled them to make spectacular debuts in the pro game, Richardson's rookie miseries were business as usual.

But he spent the summer in Denver working out ten hours every day and playing in every summer league within two hundred miles. When he returned to New York for the 1979–80 season, he'd transformed himself into one of the NBA's premier guards.

Big Man in the Big Apple

"I was flat-out killing people. I really used to get jacked up against the white guards because I didn't like the straight up-and-down way they played. Maybe they reminded me of the team that beat us for the high-school championship. Or the crackers that used to bust my ass in Lubbock. It was a white world, and I was just another underdog. And even though Isiah Thomas was blacker than the inside of my ass, he had a white game, so I went after him like he'd just slapped my momma."

Indeed, Richardson took to walking up to Thomas in Detroit's locker room and saying, "I'm gonna bust your ass up tonight." And much more often than not, Richardson made his predictions come true.

Fast forward to a preseason game in 1984 when Richardson was a three-time All-Star and playing with the New Jersey Nets. Pace Mannion was Richardson's backup and says this about the game: "We were playing the Utah Jazz in Miami and it was John Stockton's rookie season. Utah's starting point guard was a black guy named Ricky Green, and Sugar played no defense against him and never even tried to score. Then Stockton replaced Green, and on the very first play, the rookie attacked Sugar's handle and stole the ball. Well, Sugar really got pissed. The next five times the Nets had possession, he backed Stockton down to the free throw line, then turned and buried soft jumpers. Literally five times in a row. Then, as he ran past Utah's bench, Sugar yelled at coach Jerry Sloan, 'Y-y-you b-b-better g-get that white b-b-boy out of here.' So Sloan yanked Stockton and put Green back in. And Sugar went back to his who-cares game.

"After the game, I went over to Stockton and said, 'The lesson I hope you learned is that white guys should never, ever even try to rip Sugar's dribble.'"

In fact, at the time, Richardson's attitude toward white opponents mirrored the racial divide in the NBA. As hard as they might play against one another, black players never exchanged hard fouls. Yet before the institution of penalties for flagrant fouls, blacks often made sure to foul white players with sufficient force to send them sprawling. Hey, no matter how hard the contact, the officials could only call one foul per hit.

It was also common for the brothers from both teams to party together after games. Most pointedly, according to Steve Mix who played with Detroit in the '70s, the Pistons' black players and white players were so antagonistic that the two groups never communicated and dressed in opposite sides of the locker rooms.

And the refs?

In 2007 Joseph Price and Justin Wolfers published a study based on more than a quarter of a million player-game observations over a fifteen-year period (1991–2004). They concluded that white refs, by a factor of 4 percent, called more fouls on black players than on white players and that black refs reversed the process in precisely the same proportion. Moreover, the fouls called by an all-black or all-white officiating crew were even more biased.

And since in the 2013–14 season 48.4 percent of the NBA's refs were black as opposed to 79.5 percent of the players (who logged one thousand or more minutes), the study estimated that the biased calls resulted in two games per season in which the "wrong" team won. The difference, perhaps, in positioning or even qualifying for the playoffs? As well as the subsequent rankings for the annual drafts?

While Price and Wolfers judged this bias unintentional, their findings suggested a similar subconscious racial discrimination throughout our society, from job applications to the makeup of police forces, even to a teacher's choosing which students to call on to respond to easy or difficult questions. In other words, racial bias is cultural reflex.

Nevertheless, in his second season in what the players call "The League," Micheal Ray Richardson became a superstar.

"That season and the next one were great times for this poor black boy from Pigshit, Texas," says Richardson. "Now, the New York fans and the New York press were on my side. I mean I could take a bite out of the Big Apple any time I was hungry, and I was hanging with celebrities like Reggie Jackson. Night clubs, women . . . I was living the high life and running wild all over town. Like the song says, 'Looking for love in all the wrong places.'"

Among his many other attributes, Darryl Dawkins has always been an acute observer of on-court and in-bed NBA action. "I think," he says, "that the main reason why NBA players get hooked on sex is loneliness. People usually don't think of NBA players as being lonely, but they are. The loneliness comes when you don't trust women. All the guys are constantly warning each other to be wary of bad women who are just looking to grab some of their money. Like the ones who borrow fancy clothes and jewelry from their friends so they won't look like they're on the make when they meet up with players at a club. But what they really want is to get married to single guys or get pregnant with the married guys. Either way, they're looking for a big payoff."

Dawkins recalls the story of one perpetual All-Star who had lived with a woman for several years. "She kept on nagging him to get married, but the guy kept putting her off. This only made her nagging get worse and worse until one day they got into a serious argument that forced the poor bastard to give her a gentle shove just to get her out of his face. When the bitch sued him for assaulting her, it came out that the name he knew her by wasn't her real one—and her whole history was also phony. Eventually, they settled out of court for two hundred grand."

As a result of this and similar scenarios, older and wiser players limit their womanizing to clearly defined one-night stands with beautiful women. "Then you cast about for redheads with her titties up," says Dawkins, "or big-assed blondes, or skinny brunettes, or sisters with this or that. So it's loneliness that leads to lust."

According to Dawkins, "Then, now, and forever, the NBA's pussy heaven is Salt Lake City. That's one of the main reasons why blacks want to play with the Utah Jazz. The second-best pussy capital is Atlanta, with New Orleans a close third. By far the worst place to get laid is New York City, only because the girls there can't be trusted."

When connecting with newly encountered willing women in New York, the players would keep some cash in their pockets, then give their wallets, watches, and jewelry to a less-adventurous teammate for safekeeping.

(In the 2015–16 season, Derrick Williams of the Knicks was robbed of $600,000 worth of jewelry while he was sleeping by two women he had had sex with in his apartment.)

If Richardson was sleeping with all comers, one thing he wasn't doing was indulging in any other kind of drug besides an occasional joint.

Back in the sixties, smoking reefer had several purposes: It was a groovy party drug, a communion ritual for the counterculture rebels, and, as such, also a blow against the empire. Among NBA players burning a doobie was also an act of community, albeit an exclusive one. It was also a way of passing the long hours on the road in hotel rooms: just stuff wet towels under and over the doors and puff away in safety. Watching college football games on Saturday afternoons and/or NFL games on Sundays usually attracted those teammates who indulged. And good pot was always available.

(Full disclosure: As long as the late Steve Patterson played with the Cleveland Cavaliers—1971–75—I was the team's primary source of marijuana during their trips to New York. I'd pick up Steve at the airport, take him to my apartment, where he napped and gave me the orders; then he'd squeeze one-ounce baggies into the fingers of his gloves, and we'd both proceed to the Garden of Delights.)

During Neal Walk's tenure in the NBA (1968–77), his bearded, hippie nonchalance encouraged his black teammates to accept his presence at their postgame light-ups. "Guys on both teams would gather in somebody's hotel room," he reports, "order some pizza and beer, then keep the joints and the laughter flowing. It was beautiful."

The NBA has always employed a clandestine "security" department, primarily to avoid point-shaving scandals and also to track any drug abuse and/or gambling debts that might make players vulnerable to blackmail. Despite the private claims of several players (among them Richardson, Dawkins, and Walk) that from 50 to 60 percent of NBA players were smoking marijuana on a regular basis in the later 1970s and early 1980s, twenty years later Commissioner David Stern downplayed the adverse effect on the league. "Initially we went through a period of 'Oh, my goodness,'" said Stern. "But we eventually came to understand it's a reflection of society." Stern conceded that drugs were once a problem for the league but no longer a serious threat. "Nowadays we see ourselves as fighting a small portion of a larger problem."

Whatever that means.

However, once cocaine replaced pot as the NBA players' drug of choice, Stern's rather dismissive attitude became much more aggressive. And before long Richardson was in Stern's crosshairs. Ah, but like so many NBA hooplings, Sugar Ray believed he was invulnerable. His youth would last forever. The riches of the world, of *his* world, were inexhaustible. The drugs stretched the party of his life into infinity, while beautiful women beyond counting begged to be fucked.

Meanwhile, within the safe confines of the court, Richardson scored 15.3 points per game and led the NBA in both assists (10.1 per game) and steals (2.23 per game), compelling Holzman to increase his average playing time to over thirty-seven minutes. Micheal Ray's sterling play was officially acknowledged by his appearance in the 1980 All-Star Game. (His stats in that elite if casual competition included 13 minutes played, 3-7 shooting, 1 rebound, 2 assists, and 6 points.) In addition, Richardson was later named to the NBA's All-Defense First Team.

There's no doubt that while Richardson was indeed one of the league's premier defenders, it should be noted that most of the NBA's postseason awards are questionable at best. For example, Kobe Bryant, Karl Malone, David Robinson, Mark Eaton, Manute Bol, Shaquille O'Neal, and Dwight Howard have all been named to the All-Defense First Team on numerous occasions. In truth, Robinson, Eaton, Shaq, Bol, and Howard had difficulty defending any opponent who could turn-face-and-shoot. What they could do, though, was come from the weak side, block shots, and intimidate others—a skill set that too many of the writers and broadcasters who vote for this award confuse with actually playing defense.

While a shot smacked into the high-priced seats might be dramatic, the smackee's team retains possession. Plus, Howard and Robinson were so focused on blocks that smart opponents could easily sucker them to the ball, then make slick passes to the neglected big men they were supposed to be guarding for unopposed layups and dunks.

Moreover, although blocks are meaningful, they are not the end all and be all of good defense. Back in the days before blocked shots became an official statistic, intrepid sportswriters would sometimes track the shots blocked by Bill Russell and Wilt Chamberlain. Their average in select games would range from ten to fifteen. Nowadays, a player averaging three plus per game is usually enough to lead the league. In truth, alert and timely rotations have much more significant impacts on ball games.

As for Malone and Bryant . . . the former was strong enough to bully opponents off of prime position in the low post; otherwise his defense consisted of gambling to intercept entry passes and/ or swiping at the ball while his opposite number raised the ball to launch a shot. More often than not, these gambles resulted in unchallenged shots for the bad guys.

Bryant's primary defensive tactic was to abandon his man and follow the bouncing ball looking for steals and breakaway dunkers. Snappy ball movement by the opposing teams would easily locate the left-open man and result in an uncontested shot or a foul on one of Kobe's teammates.

And here's the kicker: in 2012 the writers and broadcasters made Tyson Chandler the Defensive Player of the Year. Meanwhile, in a vote of the league's coaches, Chandler was relegated to the All-Defense Second Team.

Another postseason honor that's even more bogus is the Most Valuable Player award. Just what does this award actually mean? That the recipient is the best player in the league? Since every player has a different role on his team, perhaps a game of one on one would be the only way to determine this. But what if the candidates are, say, a big lumbering center and a swift point guard, each with vastly different responsibilities? Nor are statistics any kind of realistic measure for determining the identity of an MVP. In most cases the award is presented to the "best" player on the best team. But what about somebody like Kobe Bryant with the woeful 2012–13 Lakers? Subtract him and, instead of (barely) making the playoffs, the Lakers would have finished at the bottom of the league. Is that valuable enough?

Perhaps the best definition of MVP comes from a mysterious Tweeter whose handle is "Old Hoss Radbourne," which is the name of a durable Major League pitcher in the late nineteenth century: "My criterion for most valuable is the player whose kidnapping would net the most money."

Other postseason awards are even more dubious. Phil Jackson is a certified Hall of Fame coach, having won a record eleven championships. Yet he was awarded one solitary coach of the year award (for the 1995–96 season). How could this be? Because the players at his command included Michael Jordan and Scottie Pippen in Chicago, plus Shaquille O'Neal and Kobe Bryant in Los Angeles. And, the attitude of the media Muppets who voted was, How could Jackson's teams not win with such outstanding players at his command? All he had to do was roll the ball out on to the court and let MJ, Pip, Shaq, and Kobe do their thing, right?

Wrong. In fact it's extremely difficult to win when you're "supposed" to win. Colossal superstars invariably have colossal egos that a coach has to carefully nurture. Other season-long chores that concerned Jackson was battling any feeling of complacency, of cruising through games with the belief that they could turn on their collective and individual A games in the clutch. All the while, establishing and maintaining the undivided attention of his players.

Plus, Jordan had been in the NBA for five ringless seasons before Jackson took over the Bulls—winning his initial championship in MJ's sixth season. Pippen was a two-year NBA vet before winning his first ring in his fourth season under PJ. Kobe and Shaq totaled ten fruitless NBA campaigns until Jackson led them to the title in his first season in Los Angeles.

And if any combination of super-duper stars is sufficient to win a championship, why didn't the otherwise transcendent trio of Jerry West, Elgin Baylor, and Wilt Chamberlain ever attain this goal?

Here's another egregious miscall by the writers and broadcasters: In 2000 Jason Kidd won the Pacific Division's sportsmanship award. This, despite the fact that when Kidd, Jim Jackson, and Jamaal Mashburn were teammates with the 1996–97 Dallas Mavericks, they refused to pass the ball to one another because they were all sleeping with the same woman. And, of course, years later Kidd was charged with beating his wife. Then in 2013 he was suspended for the initial three games of his coaching career for a DWI arrest and conviction.

In any case, Richardson had reason to celebrate during that breakout season of 1979–80. To reward his bona fide status, he supplemented his Porsche with a BMW and a Jaguar. On off nights when the Knicks were in New York, one of Richardson's cars would be routinely parked illegally in front of the city's most exclusive nightclubs. His celebrity insured that he never received a parking ticket.

The 1980-81 season brought more hoop-time glory for Richardson: 16.4 points, 7.9 assists, and 6.9 rebounds in 40.2 minutes per game. Plus another appearance in the All-Star Game, as well as repeating as an NBA All-Defense First Teamer.

Aside from being a good shooter and spectacular finisher, Richardson had quick hands, quick feet, long limbs, as well as the ability to see a game unfold a heartbeat faster than anybody else on the court. Plus he was more brash, restless, and bold than cooler-than-thou NBA stars were supposed to be. His peers had total respect for Richardson. Magic Johnson said that Micheal Ray always came right at him: "He talked plenty of trash but he always was able to back it up." Isiah Thomas once told a sportswriter that Richardson was the one opponent he was afraid to face. Buck Williams spoke of Richardson's ability to deliver in the clutch, saying, "In the last two minutes, it's his game." Michael Jordan claimed there were only two players that he hated to play against: A tough defensive specialist named Alvin Robertson . . . and Micheal Ray Richardson.

An underground New York newspaper, *Weekly Soho News*, put Richardson on a cover that anointed him "THE GREAT BLACK HOPE."

All this as one of his teammates introduced Richardson to the dubious pleasures of snorting coke. At the time, research by the *Los Angeles Times* found that 75 percent of NBA players were using cocaine.

His new-found habit explains why Richardson was so exuberant after every victory and so animatedly distressed after every loss. Win or lose, his postgame behavior was so over the top that his teammates tried in vain to calm him down.

Coach Hubie Brown was destined for the Naismith Hall of Fame, but during the 1980–81 season, he discovered that the roster of his Atlanta Hawks was top heavy with drug abusers. "I'm naive," he says. "I never smoked a joint or did coke. I never needed that stuff. At the same time, one of the principal rules of leadership is to realize that you can't attack negative behavior without understanding it. So I paid $1,200 out of my own pocket to consult a pro. I didn't want to lose a damn ball game when I needed thirty-two minutes of all-out play from a guy who could only give me twenty-four because of drugs. So I learned the reasons and methods of drug use."

Brown learned that NBA players sniffed cocaine after games for two main reasons: To prolong that razor-edge of physical, emotional, and mental awareness that was necessary for them to compete against the world's greatest hoopers. And to maintain that same sharpness when engaging in after-game sex.

"Most of all," says Brown, "I learned to recognize the symptoms of drug abuse."

As a result, Brown would often confront a player he was positive was using coke, going so far as grabbing him by the throat and shoving him forcefully against a locker. But the players just laughed at Brown. And when Brown took his complaints to Ted Turner, the team's owner downplayed the use of coke as being a recreational drug.

Brown was fired after that dismal season and set up shop behind a microphone, doing color commentary of NBA telecasts until returning to coach the Knicks (1982–87). Another stint as a sportscaster led to his being hired to coach Memphis Grizzlies (2002–5).

After his stellar 1980–81 season, Richardson made a fateful decision. Instead of returning to Denver during the summer, he decided to stay in New York. During that time, the Knicks made several roster moves. The ones that impacted Richardson the most was parting company with his two closest friends on the team—Mike Glenn and Ray Williams. The news devastated Richardson, and the agenda of his new circle of friends did not include basketball.

"One night I was with some women and some guys from Trinidad, just drinking and partying. Then one of them brought out a sack of coke. I did some serious sniffing but to no effect. It was simply some bullshit stuff. Two weeks later, I came across the same folks again and this time they showed me how to freebase. Man! That shit was goooood!

"That first hit felt like the best thing that ever happened to me, and the best thing that could ever happen to me. I was invisible and invincible. On top of the world. Every worry that was buzzing around in my mind was instantly gone. Responsibility didn't mean a thing. It was a freaky drug experience with all of my fantasies becoming possible. I could get it on with three or four girls at a time and go at it all night long. Man! I barely knew who I was, only that whoever I was I was king of the fucking world. Make that king of the universe. I spent the next seven years trying to duplicate that very first high. And from the get-go, basketball didn't seem as important as getting off.

"Coming down was a bitch, though. I'd get depressed. What the fuck did I do? Where the fuck was I? How much money had I spent? A gram cost a hundred dollars and would last for about two hours. My only consolation was that about one out of every three players in the NBA was also freebasing, so once the season started, there were high-time parties going on in every city in the league."

Prompted by his drug buddies, Richardson began haunting the drug houses. "Racing up flights of stairs past junkies nodding on the landings. The peep hole in the door. Three guys sitting at a table, each one holding an Uzi. Then I'd make my transaction and they'd push me out the door. They knew who I was, but I didn't give a fuck. They even charged me less. That's when I failed my first drug test."

Under the rules then on the books, Richardson was assessed a first strike and issued a warning that another positive test would compel him to enroll in a rehab program. But Richardson couldn't stop freebasing.

Even so, Richardson's numbers for the 1981–82 season were still admirable—17.9 points, 7.0 assists, and 6.9 rebounds per game. Good enough to merit a third All-Star Game appearance. But he was increasingly careless with the ball and guilty of too many unforced turnovers. His defense also suffered, to the point where Isiah Thomas was no longer afraid of him—and Micheal Ray would never again be voted to either the All-Defense first or even second team.

Yet despite his lack of focus and declining interest in basketball, Richardson still had several highly impressive performances: "We were playing a Sunday afternoon home game against Houston, and I'd gotten so high that I completely forgot about the game. I'd been up all night, and I'd just smoked a bowl at 8:35 a.m. when I suddenly remembered that in less than five hours I'd be playing in a nationally televised game! Fuck me! So I took a long hot shower, and since freebasing is very dehydrating, I drank a quart of orange juice. I got to the Garden at ten thirty, took another hot shower, gulped down another quart of orange juice, ate two bacon-and-egg sandwiches, and suddenly it was time to start our warm-ups. While I was loosening up, I kept telling myself that I'd never do this again. 'Please, God. Get me out of this one and I'll go cold turkey. I'll check into a rehab clinic. I'll do anything. Then I went out and had me a triple-double. So I got stoned for the next twenty-four hours."

And if Richardson still had sufficient awareness to be the Knicks' high scorer, the 1981–82 squad featured the underwhelming likes of Bill Cartwright, aka "Medical Bill" because of his chronic injuries; the declining talents of Maurice Lucas; the last gasp of both Campy Russell and Randy Smith; journeyman Sly Williams; as well as Marvin Webster, who might have had the worst hands in NBA history. In Red Holzman's last season occupying the command seat, the Knicks were fortunate to win thirty-three games.

Then, in a postgame interview, Richardson's midseason analysis of the team's condition became perhaps the most famous quote in the history of the league:

Q: What do you think is happening to this team?
A: The ship be sinking.
Q: How far can it sink?
A: The sky's the limit.

At the time, Richardson said that he was quoted out of context, a claim that smacked of a desperate and flimsy self-defense. These days Richardson stands by the line. "At the time we were sinking." And he can now look back on his infamous interview with a sense of humor: "What I should've done was get a patent on it, like Pat Riley did with 'three-peat.' Then I would've been rich."

Years later, an agent for the Federal Bureau of Investigation publically claimed that there might have been more nefarious ways that Richardson had actually enriched himself during that 1981–82 season.

To Fix or Not to Fix, That Was the Question

According to documents cited by author Brian Tuohy in *Larceny Games: Sports Gambling, Game Fixing and the FBI*, the Federal Bureau of Investigation had investigated widespread suspicions that three Knicks were shaving points. All three were described as "heavy users of cocaine" and were suspected of being in league with their coke supplier, cited as being "one of the largest dealers on the East Coast," to unduly influence the outcome of certain games.

The dealer was a degenerate gambler who usually bet $300 a game, informants told the investigators, but in January 1982 he began laying $10,000 wagers on Knicks opponents—and winning. By March 25, the coke dealer had won six of his seven-figure bets against the Knicks—while continuing to make his normal $300 wagers on other NBA games.

One of the FBI's informants told the feds that one of the Knicks owed a "large . . . gambling debt" to a Lucchese family bookie. At the same time, FBI agents began to suspect that in the latter part of the season the three Knicks had bet several games "against themselves." Their suspicion was validated by an unnamed source who reported that in each game that the Knicks trio had bet on their opponents, "the Knicks did lose, or failed to cover the point spread."

Richardson was the most obvious suspect. "Hell, no," he said when *Larceny Games* was released in September 2013. "We never did anything like that."

But without any physical evidence—and no confessions—the FBI closed the investigation in 1986 without making any arrests.

Even as the FBI's investigation was in full swing, the FBI and the NBA initiated the Sports Presentation Program, sending agents to teams to warn the players of the dangers inherent in gambling.

"It was no coincidence," said Tuohy.

Whether the three Knicks did or did not conspire to fix games, the NBA has a long history of players and referees turning tricks for gamblers.

Flash back to April 13, 1947, when the Basketball Association of America (which wouldn't become the NBA until 1949) was completing its inaugural season. The Chicago Stags had just closed out the semifinal playoff series by upsetting the highly favored Washington Capitals in six games. Here's the testimony of Johnny Norlander, one of the Caps' starting guards: "There were several reasons why we lost. First off, we were fatigued. And secondly, because Red [Auerbach] never developed his bench players. But there was a third reason that was more important than the others. [In the sixth and final game] we were up by six points with only a couple of minutes to go, and we could taste the win. But from there until the end, the Stags made a parade to the foul line. In fact, they failed to notch a single field goal during that stretch. Just about all of the calls that sent them to the line were clearly ridiculous ones, and they were all made by the same ref: Nat Messenger. The other ref was Pat Kennedy, a guy I knew from the games he worked when I was in college. Pat was always a straight arrow, and the two of them had reffed every single game in the series, all six of them. As we walked off the court after the final buzzer, Kennedy nodded at Messenger and said to me, 'Wasn't that terrible?' All I could do was to sadly agree."

It was well known that Messenger habitually associated with notorious gamblers, but both the players and the league officials believed that his social life was his own business. However, that August several detectives hired by the league made a startling discovery. Here's Norlander again: "That's when we found out that Messenger had a substantial amount of money bet on Chicago to win the series. . . . We felt like the series, and the championship, were stolen from us by a crooked ref."

It was too late to change the outcome, but Messenger never worked another Basketball Association of America or NBA game.

Salvatore Sollazzo was the gambler who was responsible for paying several key players at City College of New York, Long Island University (LIU), and New York University to shave points in the late 1940s and early 1950s. His point man was Eddie Gard, a talented player for the LIU Blackbirds who knew everybody who was anybody in the New York City basketball universe. Among Gard's acquaintances was Sol Levy, who had been an assistant coach at LIU before World War II. In addition to working for an advertising agency in Brooklyn, Levy was also an NBA referee during the 1950–51 season. Since Levy's NBA annual salary was a meager $3,000, he easily succumbed to a deal offered by Gard and Sollazzo—to control the point spreads in selected NBA games for $1,000 per game.

When Sollazzo and his ring of point shavers and game fixers were finally uncovered, he was quick to give up Levy. Eventually, Levy was convicted of altering the scores of three NBA games that were played in November of 1950. His conviction was overturned because of some arcane technicality, but Levy's officiating career was defunct.

Gard served time in prison, while Sollazzo, who was not an American citizen, was deported to Italy.

Jack Molinas was a rookie with the 1953–54 Fort Wayne Pistons. Even though he routinely shaved points at Columbia University (and even in high school!), Molinas was an extraordinary player. During a game in Syracuse against the Nationals, three of the Pistons' key players had played poorly, but Molinas's heroics in the fourth quarter nearly salvaged a win for the visitors. Knowing the theory and practice of fixing ballgames, Molinas approached this trio after the game and said this: "Hey, guys. I know you're dumping and I want in." Indeed, Molinas had demonstrated that the Pistons games could not be fixed unless he was involved, so he was gladly accepted into the clique.

By no means, though, was this an isolated incident. In the late '40s and early '50s, George Mikan was the league's highest-paid player, earning $12,000 annually from the Minneapolis Lakers. Bob Cousy and Dolph Schayes each made an estimated $7,500. "All the rest of us," said an ex-NBAer who played from 1949 to 1953, "got paid about thirty-five hundred bucks plus seven bucks a day for meals on the road, and, believe me, it wasn't easy to live on that kind of money, especially if you had a wife and kids. . . . A lot of good players couldn't afford to play in the NBA. At the same time there were no other career options available to us. We had to make a living, you know? And that's why so many NBA players when I was playing were doing business."

Like who?

"Like almost all the players on the Baltimore Bullets," says one veteran of that team. "There was another player, a big man, who occasionally played to lose. When his teammates figured out what he was doing they were pissed. Oh, shit. There he goes again. Instead of throwing him catchable passes, they'd throw passes at his ankles just to make him look clumsy. Who else? A bunch of guys on the Knicks, especially the players who came from New York."

Whitey Von Nieda, who played for three seasons with the old Tri-Cities Blackhawks, recalled several teammates who studied the point spreads printed in the newspapers "like other guys studied the Bible."

Another one-time pro said this: "Even after the college scandals broke, there were plenty of games dumped in the NBA. One of my teammates was a famous superstar who had an unstoppable pet move to the basket. Whenever he was doing business, he would take three dribbles away from the basket and throw up a wild hook shot. That was the signal that he was on board. We heard that he was making half his yearly salary every time he fixed a game."

In 1954 the New York district attorney Frank Hogan came to NBA commissioner Maurice Podoloff with hard evidence that one superstar player was in league with gamblers. When Hogan demanded that the player be booted from the league, the owner of the team threatened to fold his franchise if Podoloff ever dared to even question his best player, and the star remained in orbit.

After the 1951 scandals, the NBA's sleuths began eavesdropping on the telephone calls of virtually every player in the league. So it was that Jack Molinas was banned from the NBA in January 1954 for repeatedly betting on his own team to win—which wasn't exactly the truth. But to reveal that Molinas was, in fact, betting against the Pistons would have done irreparable damage to the credibility of the NBA.

For the same reason, several other veteran players—many of them bona fide All-Stars—who were also turning tricks for gamblers got a pass. But Molinas was a mere rookie and from an Ivy League college to boot, so he was deemed to be expendable.

Here's Molinas's version of part of a conversation he had with Podoloff, whom he usually referred to as "Poodles." Molinas's purpose was to try to convince Podoloff to rescind the banishment.

"Mister Podoloff, surely you must know that there are players on the Fort Wayne team that were shaving points and dumping games."

"I'm aware of that," said Podoloff.

"Then how can you come down so hard on me just for betting on my team to win?"

"You're a first-year player, Jack, and if I were to get anybody in trouble who's been playing in the league for several years, it might hurt the structure of the league."

"What if I held a press conference and exposed the names of all the players who were doing business with gamblers? What if I gave out specific names and dates? What if I brought a big-time gambler to the press conference to back up all of my charges? I'm telling you, Mister Podoloff, I'm fully prepared to do this unless I'm immediately readmitted."

"I will not make any deals, Jack. Be certain about that. And, yes, you could hold your press conference and tell your dirty stories and even bring in your so-called witness. But it wouldn't do you any good, Jack. First of all, it would put the absolute final seal on your dismissal from the league. Secondly, the league would certainly take a hit, but in the long run we would survive simply because the public likes our product. And thirdly, no one would believe you, Jack. You'd only be making a fool of yourself."

Molinas had no choice but to agree with Podoloff. His dream of continuing his NBA career was over, but not his interest in fixing games.

Indeed, his banishment did not stop Molinas from betting on Piston games, nor did it discourage his former teammates from continuing to conspire with gamblers.

Here's the testimony of a one-time NBA player: "Jack took the brunt of the whole thing, and the other Fort Wayne players had to make sure that he wouldn't rat on them so they kept him informed whenever they were doing business. Anyway, shortly after he was barred from the league, the Pistons were playing the Knicks, and me and Jack were sitting in the balcony and watching the game. New York was favored by two and a half points, and Jack's ex-teammates had informed him to bet on the Knicks. Which we both did.

"Anyway, there's about two minutes left in the game, Fort Wayne was neck-and-neck with the Knicks, and I was shitting in my BVDs. 'Jack,' I said. 'We're losing.' And he said, 'Don't worry.' But nothing happened. The Pistons were still playing like they wanted to win the game. 'Jack,' I said, 'there's only one minute to go and we're going to lose.' 'Don't worry,' he repeated. Now there's only thirty seconds on the clock, the score is tied, and I was going crazy. I'd bet the rent money, the money to pay for my car payments, the money for my electric bill. 'Jack!' I said. But he was still calm as could be. 'Don't worry,' he said.

"Then all of a sudden, one of the Pistons was dribbling the ball in the backcourt all by himself. I mean his defender was about fifteen feet away and the guy just kicked the ball out of bounds. It almost looked like a football player drop-kicking the ball. Now the Knicks had the ball and another one of the Pistons made a clumsy effort to steal the ball and instead committed an obvious foul. The Knicks made both free throws, they're up by two, the Pistons had the ball, and there seemed to be no way New York's going to cover the two and a half. The clock was ticking down . . . ten . . . nine . . . eight. If the Pistons scored a basket, I was a loser. If the Pistons didn't score, I still lost. 'Jack! I'm dying!' 'Don't worry.'

"There's five seconds to go when we heard somebody on the Pistons' bench shout out loud, 'You motherfucking referee!'

Bang! The ref called a technical foul, the Knicks made the shot and won the game by three points! And Jack turned to me with a shit-eating grin on his face. 'I told you not to worry,' he said."

Early in the 1957–58 season, the NBA secretly informed every team that their surveillance of several players had continued. Phones were tapped. Hotel rooms were bugged. The league knew that certain players had been, and still were, doing business with gamblers. The NBA suggested that if the players in question (who were not specifically named) would quietly retire at the end of the season they would not face public charges. At the end of that 1957–58 season, several players who had plenty of game left retired prematurely. Among them were three of Molinas's ex-teammates, Mel Hutchins, Don Meineke, and future Hall of Famer Andy Phillip.

NBA action was apparently honest and above board for several years thereafter. Then on January 7, 1973, the Philadelphia 76ers visited the Seattle SuperSonics. The 76ers were a pitiful crew and coached by Roy Rubin, absolutely the worst coach in the history of the NBA. At the time, Philadelphia's record was 3-38, on their way to an infamous season's mark of 9-73. Not that the host team was much better.

The Sonics had a record of 13-31, and coach Tom Nissalke was a notorious martinet, always demanding absolute perfection and verbally abusing his players when they failed to measure up to his often unobtainable standards. There was a gross mismatch between the nit-picking Nissalke and the Sonics roster that was top heavy with immature, malcontented, and even belligerent players: the likes of John Brisker, Spencer Haywood, Jim McDaniels, and Dontonio Winfield. At various times, Nissalke had tried benching them, fining them, lecturing them, threatening them, and cajoling them, but chronic lateness to and/or missed practices and extremely selfish and/or lackadaisical play continued. As much as Nissalke disliked many of his players, the feeling was mutual.

According to Nissalke, the media on hand, and the visiting team, the Sonics saw the game against the hapless 76ers as an opportunity to embarrass their coach and get him fired by deliberately tanking the game. Against the worst defensive team in the league, Brisker (who averaged 12.8 points for the season) scored a solitary bucket; Haywood tallied 18, over 11 points below his seasonal average. And the Sixers won.

Three days later, Nissalke was indeed fired.

Before and after that game, there have always been widespread rumors that certain teams had tanked entire seasons in order to be awarded a number-one draft pick (or, in some seasons, to be one of the two teams with the worst records to engage in a coin toss for this coveted pick). Indeed, this is precisely why the NBA brain trust instituted the lottery system in 1985.

As recently as November 2013, the possibility resurfaced of NBA teams low gearing their way through a season in order to increase the odds of their drafting blue-chip college players. This discussion came after star-spangled performances by Andrew Wiggens, Jabari Parker, and Julius Randle in a Kansas-Duke matchup. All three were projected as being perennial NBA All-Stars and franchise players. Yet, even as the idea of tanking was proposed, it was universally condemned.

However, just the mere mention of such a practice demonstrated the viability of its being exercised.

In the spring of 1991, ESPN presented the blackened profile and voice-altered testimony of a player who had been part of a recent NCAA championship team. The anonymous player swore that several of his teammates who were currently playing in the NBA had been periodically shaving points during their college careers. No denials were ever forthcoming.

Shortly thereafter, and on the heels of a tragic murder, the rumor of the possibility of the NBA's best player fixing games gained enormous traction: Michael Jordan never made any excuses for his lust for gambling. That's why he never denied running up a debt of $1.25 million to a San Diego businessman named Richard Esquinas during a ten-day gambling-golfing marathon. Even though Esquinas was later convicted of dealing cocaine, the NBA never seriously investigated this situation.

In any event, the rumor proposed that Jordan had lost several million dollars over the course of his frequent visits to the casino in Atlantic City. Since MJ was reluctant to settle his debts over the summer of 1993, the Atlantic City mafia allegedly offered him three choices: pay the money immediately, conspire with them to fix the outcome of Bulls games . . . and the third option was "or else."

Jordan turned down the first pair of options, and in the following October, Jordan's beloved father was gunned down while driving on a back road. The official investigation claimed that "two thugs" were the killers, but conspiracy buffs deemed the investigation to be only superficial.

Only Jordan and several underworld characters know if this scenario is true or false.

Given all the facts and rumors of payoffs from gamblers to players, the NBA seemed to change its definition of what exactly constituted sufficient grounds for the banishment of a player either suspected, or even proven, to have been engaged with "doing business."

Ralph Beard and Alex Groza led the University of Kentucky to NCAA championships in 1948 and 1949. Moreover, Beard and Groza were also instrumental in leading the U.S. squad to a gold medal in the 1948 Olympic Games. Both turned pro in 1949, signing with the Indianapolis Olympians, the first and only NBA team that was owned and operated by its players. And both had tremendous success: Beard was a point guard who, over the course of his only two NBA seasons, averaged 15.9 points and 4.4 assists. Groza played center, and over the same period his numbers were even more impressive—22.5 points and 10.7 rebounds per game. No wonder both were deemed to be among the league's best players, with Groza an NBA All-Star in 1950 and 1951, and Beard joining him in 1951.

Then, before the start of the 1951–52 season, Beard and Groza were arrested and charged with accepting money from gamblers to fix games while playing at Kentucky. Subsequently, Podoloff banned both of them from the NBA.

Groza never refuted the charge, but Beard did. He swore to several writers (including me) that while he had indeed accepted money from gamblers, he had never done anything to alter the outcome of any game. Given that Beard was such a ferocious competitor and grew up in dire poverty, it's easy to believe his story. In fact, there was never any proof that Beard was either an actual fixer or dumper.

So, the fact that he pocketed the money was enough for him to be banished from the NBA.

Fast forward to March 27, 1985, when John "Hot Rod" Williams, an All-American forward at Tulane, was arrested on suspicion of point shaving. Williams readily admitted that he had received at least $8,500 from a well-known gambler named Gary Kranz in return for influencing point spreads in games against Southern Mississippi, Memphis State, and Virginia Tech. Williams was charged with sports bribery and conspiracy. His first appearance in court resulted in a mistrial. During a subsequent trial, Williams testified that, although he did accept and keep the money, he never played less than his best during those games.

So, whereas Williams went on to have a long (1986–99) and successful NBA career, Ralph Beard's professional career was aborted for committing the same "crime."

And, of course, any discussion of real, suspected, and chimerical point shaving in the NBA must include the testimony of Tim

Donaghy—a one-time NBA referee who admitted to betting on games he worked but denied altering any outcomes thereof. Rare is the NBA watcher who is so naive as to believe that Donaghy never called invisible fouls on star players and made spurious determinations of other infractions to insure that his bets would be fruitful.

So then, if Micheal Ray Richardson did not fix any games during that 1981–82 season, then the FBI spokesman misspoke. But if Sugar Ray did, then he was part of a long, dishonored NBA tradition.

Moving from Coast to Coast to Coast

After the Knicks' disastrous 33-49 performance during the 1981–82 season, Hubie Brown replaced Red Holzman. Brown was a superb technician who had broken the game down into every conceivable situation: How to execute and defend single-double baseline picks. How to throw lob passes into pivot men. Which was the push-off foot for making a zipper cut from here and also from there. Which way to turn when slipping a pick and roll. Letting the defense determine if a shooter should curl, fade, or make a back-door cut when presented with a down pick. And so on.

On the other side of the ledger, Brown was an unbending perfectionist who was quick to curse any player who zigged when he should have zagged. Players chaffed under this constant and often vicious verbal abuse. They also resented Brown's insistence that he, not any of the players, was the star of the team.

Because Brown also had a cast eye, his players ridiculed him in private: Instead of being an NBA coach, he was best suited to be a lookout on a battleship during wartime when he could watch for hostile submarines and airplanes without moving his head. Micheal Ray had a simpler way of describing Brown: "He's a google-eyed motherfucker."

After Brown's experience with druggies in Atlanta, he wanted nothing to do with Richardson. Since Bernard King had left Golden State to sign a free-agent contract with the Knicks, Richardson was sent to the Warriors as compensation.

A player's reaction to getting traded can range from depression to euphoria. Moving from a losing team to a winner or vice versa are critical factors. Other vital considerations are the addition or reduction in playing time, any changes in the player's accustomed role, the theories and practices of his new coach, the friendliness or enmity that may have been established with his new teammates, and the lifestyle available in his new home. While some players are upset at not being wanted by their former team, this feeling of betrayal is usually trumped by the new team's enthusiastic welcome.

All things considered, then, Richardson should have been delighted by the move. After all the Knicks were 33-49 in 1981–82 while the Warriors were 45-37. So, too, Golden State's holdover point guard was the decidedly mediocre Lorenzo Romar. And if San Francisco lacked the glamour of New York, it was still an exciting place to live. Plus, Richardson had no desire to play under Hubie Brown. Even so, Micheal Ray didn't report to Golden State for a couple of months.

"While my agent was trying to squeeze more money out of the Warriors," says Richardson, "I stayed in New York smoking my brains out, running the streets at night, hanging with all of the city's sports heroes one night, then hanging out with the worst kind of street scum the next night. The worst part was that I was thinking everything was cool. I wasn't an addict, I was just having myself a good time. When we finally got the deal done with Golden State, I went out there and sprained my ankle the first day I practiced. So now I was holed up and all strung out in a Holiday Inn. Women were bringing me drugs and food, and I was totally fucked up. This was the low point in my life so far."

Al Attles had been Golden State's coach since 1970, after playing eleven seasons as a rough-and-tumble-in-your-face point guard for the Warriors in both their incarnations in Philadelphia and in California. For the 1982–83 season, Attles joined Paul Silas in San Diego and Lenny Wilkens in Seattle as being the only black coaches in the twenty-three-team league.

(Fast forward to the 2012–13 season when twelve of the NBA's thirty teams were coached by black men. But by 2016–17, there were only eight black coaches in the league.)

Eventually Richardson's ankle healed, and he managed to get back into playing shape. "But if I didn't have any problems with my teammates," he says, "I had a hard time with Al Attles, my latest coach. Even though Attles was the blackest motherfucker anybody ever saw, he was nothing but an Uncle Tom. He was a yes-man in the organization, he didn't know the game, and he was the worst coach I ever played for."

To make matters worse, Richardson and wife divorced. Plus, during his time in San Francisco, he spent almost $50,000 on his drugs of choice. If Richardson made sure to be straight during games, he would frequently lose his concentration. "I'd forget what I was supposed to do," he said.

No wonder Richardson played poorly. His per game averages included 12.5 points (his lowest total since his rookie season) and a career-low shooting percentage of .412. He did manage, though, to dish out 7.4 assists and make 3.1 steals. After thirty-three games, Richardson was traded to the New Jersey Nets for Mickey Johnson and Sleepy Floyd.

Coaching the Nets was Larry Brown, a graduate of North Carolina who, because of his penchant for thinking that the next job on the horizon was the better than the one he had, was dubbed "Next Town Brown." The itinerary of Brown's complete coaching history reads like a madcap, hop-scotching hoops travelogue: Raleigh, North Carolina (ABA); Denver; Los Angeles (at UCLA);

New Jersey; Lawrence, Kansas; San Antonio; Los Angeles (with the Clippers); Indiana; Philadelphia; Detroit; New York; and Dallas (at Southern Methodist University). Through it all, Brown was impatient, a chronic nagger, demanding (except for players from the Atlantic Coast Conference), and alternately enthusiastic and cynical. After games, Brown's posture was usually either "I won" or "They lost." During what was left of the 1982–83 season, Brown was also Richardson's latest substitute father.

"I knew Larry from when he coached the Denver team in the ABA [American Basketball Association]. I was still in high school, and he used to let me watch the Nuggets' practices and leave me tickets for their games. I was so happy to be back in the New York area that I stopped getting high. I was straight for the rest of the season, which amounted to three months."

As for Brown, he said that he would judge Micheal Ray for himself.

Richardson told Brown only that he was having "personal problems" and "financial trouble." Brown's assessment was that Richardson was depressed and had no self-esteem.

Even though Richardson prided himself on being drug free, he was still bedding down as many women as he could. Before one game, Micheal Ray said this to Fred Kerber, a sportswriter for the *New York Post*: "I'm gonna have a great game because my sperm count is very low."

Despite his drug-free and sperm-reduced condition, many of Richardson's numbers continued to dive. Although he scored 12.7 points per game for the Nets, his assists were down to 6.0, and his steals to 2.6. Remarkably, Richardson still paced the NBA in steals with an overall season's average of 2.84.

But if Richardson had taken steps to straighten out his life, Brown was up to his old crooked tricks. The Nets were playing well, and Brown gave them a Sunday and Monday off prior to a practice on Tuesday. On Wednesday they were scheduled to fly to

Detroit. Mike Weber was a reporter for the *Newark Star-Ledger*, and he heard a rumor that Brown was in Kansas City about to be interviewed for the coaching job at the University of Kansas. Somehow Webber found the hotel and the room number where Brown was staying, so he made a phone call.

"Hello?"

"Hello? May I speak to John Williams, please?"

"There's no John Williams here, but this is Larry Brown."

"Hi, Larry. This is Mike Webber from the *Star-Ledger*."

BLAM! Brown hung up the phone in a hurry. But now the news was out.

Brown was back in New Jersey for Tuesday's practice, but when he took it easy on his players, they knew that something was up. After an early morning meeting with the Nets' owner, Joe Taub, Brown was still with the team when they prepared to board the plane to Detroit. Then Taub appeared, pulled Brown aside, and fired him on the spot.

Since Joe Taub placed such a high value on loyalty (as Richardson would personally experience later on), he felt that Brown had betrayed him when he interviewed for another job while still under contract with the Nets.

According to Darryl Dawkins, only Richardson and the Nets' two ACC players (Albert King and Buck Williams) missed Brown. "The rest of us," says Dawkins, "were glad to see him go."

Indeed, Richardson was so upset to lose still another father figure that he resumed his snorting and smoking of cocaine.

Assistant coach Bill Blair took over, and the team finished the regular season at 2-4. Although Richardson had a brilliant series, the Nets were then were swept by the Knicks in the playoffs.

On April 1 the *New York Daily News*, noting that he had been seen in several coke houses, reported that Richardson had a drug problem. Six weeks later, he accrued strike two after failing another drug test and entered a drug rehabilitation center, Fair Oaks Hospital in Summit, New Jersey. The program was scheduled to last about seven weeks, but Richardson stayed in the clinic for only thirteen days.

"I checked myself out," he says, "because the program was bullshit. They had locked doors like a prison, and there was nothing for any of us to do except have group therapy sessions. That's where everybody was supposed to talk about their problems, but all everybody did was blame somebody else for their addictions. Their parents, their bosses, and their jobs. Shit, when I said that I did drugs because I like it, they all thought that I was crazy. Like every other drug rehab center I've ever been in this one was really all about making money. When somebody's insurance ran out, they boot them back into the streets whether they were ready or not."

Richardson spent the summer of 1983 in New York and was soon back on the pipe. Another failed drug test was amnestied because the latest collective-bargaining agreement between the NBA and the NBA Players Association would not take effect until the beginning of the 1983–84 season. Even so, Richardson was suspended without pay while he entered an NBA-sanctioned rehab program, this one at the Hazelton Foundation in Minneapolis. Upon completing the program, Richardson pronounced himself "cured."

But once the Nets' preseason workouts commenced, he was so strung out that he couldn't deal with the grueling, boring two-a-day practice sessions. After one particular exhausting day on the court, Richardson simply checked into a different hotel, summoned a few druggie friends, and was off on a crack-smoking binge that lasted four days. That's when he called a friend, Charles Grantham, who was the executive vice president of the NBA Players Association.

"I don't think basketball is for me," Richardson said. "I'll just become a truck driver."

"Just trying making it on $165 a week," said Grantham. Eventually, Grantham convinced Richardson to meet with a counselor from the Life Extension Institute, a service the league had contracted with in 1981 shortly after the *Los Angeles Times* reported that 75 percent of NBA players used cocaine. But Richardson failed to show for four different appointments. With the Nets on the verge of releasing him, however, he finally checked into still another rehab program on October 14, his third attempt at structured rehab in five months. On the day before he entered the program, Richardson and a teammate "got as high as [they] could without landing on the moon." This time, however, he completed the program and was cleaner than he had been in years.

These days, virtually every drug-abusing NBA player seeks help and rehabilitation from John Lucas, CEO of John Lucas Enterprises—and Lucas is nothing if not enterprising. Aside from his rehab work, Lucas runs a dozen skills camps throughout the year for players of all ages and levels.

As an NBA player and coach, Lucas was renowned for being a jive talker who was always upbeat and gregarious. Several ex-clients claim he tries to "bullshit" them as a way out of their addictions, but his low cure rate probably has more to do with the power of addiction than to his methodologies.

In any case, when Richardson rejoined the Nets in midseason, he had remarried and seemed to have an extremely positive attitude. However, not all of his teammates were happy to see him return to action. "If he's coming back," said Reggie Johnson, "I want to be traded." (Turned out that Johnson played out the season, his last in the NBA.) In fact, many of them remained resentful until the Nets visited the archrival New York Knicks on February 4, 1984, and Richardson bagged a three-pointer at the buzzer to give New Jersey a 108–105 win. The clutch shot set off a teamwide celebration and Richardson was back in his mates' good graces.

Playing well is always enjoyable, but above all, Richardson was thrilled to fall under the benign influence of the next on his lengthening list of coach-father figures: Stan Albeck, who was as relaxed and laid back as Larry Brown was frenetic.

For example, the Nets were down by a point with only ten seconds left in a game against the Bulls. During the timeout, Albeck designed a play to get the ball in the pivot to Dawkins. "Sugar," said Albeck as he drew lines on his game board, "I want you to dribble over to here, then dump the ball into Darryl and the game's ours. While Albeck was diagramming the play, Richardson was attentive in the huddle, nodding his head, nodding his head, and chewing on his bubble gum.

"G-got it," Richardson said. "G-got it."

Once play resumed, Dawkins ran down to his assigned spot in the pivot, and Richardson dribbled the ball to the wing just as Albeck had instructed. But instead of passing the ball to Dawkins, Richardson launched a twenty-foot jump shot. As soon as the ball left his hand, Richardson shouted, "We win!" Then while the ball was still aloft, he ran off the court toward the locker room. Of course the ball split the net.

The Nets began jumping around in celebration, and by the time they got to the locker room, Richardson was already coming out of the shower.

"I t-told you s-stupid motherfuckers we win!"

And where, despite the outcome, Larry Brown would have been hopping mad at having his instructions so blatantly ignored, Albeck just shook Richardson's hand and said, "Hell of a shot."

Another reason why Richardson and most of his teammates liked Albeck was because he was the unusual coach who liked to hang out with his players. Whereas Red Holzman told his players that the bar in whatever hotel they were quartered was his personal domain and strictly off limits to them, Albeck would routinely mingle with his charges at the hotel bars and buy drinks for all of them. And the players also liked spending some off-hours with Albeck because he had a host of funny anecdotes to share.

Like the time Albeck was an assistant when Wilt Chamberlain was the head coach of the ABA's San Diego Conquistadors. On the afternoon before a home game, Wilt told Albeck that he had a hot date with a girl who was going to be in town for only one night. Since the date and the upcoming game conflicted, Chamberlain told Albeck that he'd be late for the game. Wilt's solution was to make an audio tape of his pregame spiel and have Albeck play it in the locker room. The players laughed throughout Chamberlain's exhortation to forget about their off-court lives and to focus entirely on the game.

During that season, Joe Taub called Richardson every single day to make sure his backcourt ace was clean. "I'm cured," Richardson would reply, even though he was back on the pipe. "I was a celebrity once more," Micheal Ray recalls. "Everybody likes a comeback story, so I was bigger than ever. Once again, I was hob-nobbing with the A-list—movie stars, politicians, internationally famous athletes. But once or twice every week, I was dashing up the stairs and swivel-hipping my way past nodded-out junkies on my way to score." Still, his drug fog reduced his numbers to only 12.0 points and a 4.5 assists per game.

Otis Birdsong and Richardson composed the Nets' starting backcourt for four seasons and became the best of friends. If Birdsong believed that his buddy was clean, he was well aware that several of his teammates were freebasing. Birdsong recalled the first time he discovered this problem: "I was at a party in a teammate's house, and guys kept walking in and out of the kitchen.

So I poked my head in there and saw what they were doing. It was amazing to me that guys could do that and perform. But I never knew Micheal had that problem until everything came out in public."

Even so, the Nets finished the regular season at 45-37. But both Albeck and Taub were dismayed when the Nets ended the regular season with three losses and seemed ill prepared to enter the money season against the Philadelphia 76ers, the league's defending champs. That's why Taub was on hand during his team's initial pre-practice meeting prior to that daunting series. Taub was in total agreement when Albeck said to the players, "I'm gonna run your asses off in practice today."

This prospect did not please Richardson. "F-fuck it, man. My m-motherfucking b-body is entirely wrecked, and I ain't m-motherfucking p-practicing at all."

Taub was also so committed to helping Richardson overcome his drug problem that he ordered Albeck to cancel practice and go hard the next day. When Taub left the room, Albeck turned on Richardson. "There's a fucking asshole on every team," Albeck steamed, "and you're it."

Richardson's reaction was to stand up, drop his pants, turn away from his coach, spread his cheeks, and say, "W-well, that makes t-two of us. 'C-cause if I'm an asshole you're one t-too."

While the other players howled with laughter, Albeck merely chuckled, shook his head, and left the room.

Judging by his performance in the Philadelphia series, Richardson's body had fully recovered. He was absolutely spectacular—averaging over 20 points, 7 assists, 4 steals, and dominating virtually every clutch situation. Even though, in Julius Erving, Moses Malone, Andrew Toney, Mo Cheeks, and Bobby Jones, the 76ers' roster featured five certified All-Stars and four future Hall of Famers, Richardson led the Nets to victory in the decisive fifth game in Philadelphia.

Okay, even given Richardson's brilliance, how could the powerhouse reigning NBA champs lose in the first round? Especially with virtually a holdover roster?

The answer lies in how difficult it is for NBA champions to repeat.

Disregarding the respective dynasties of the Russellian Celtics and the Jacksonian Bulls and Lakers, only five teams have won back-to-back titles: the Mikanesque Minneapolis Lakers (twice, 1949–50 and 1953–54), the Showtime LA Lakers (1967–68), the "Bad Boy" Detroit Pistons (1989–90), the Houston Rockets (1994–95), and the Miami Heat (2012–13).

That's because defending champs tend to believe they can turn on their A games whenever necessary. Forgetting that they won their championship by playing hard and smart on every play for forty-eight minutes, their confidence borders on arrogance, and they are seldom successful.

Another factor is that championship teams play with bull's-eyes on the backs of their uniforms. Every opponent—even the league's weakest teams—get their chops up to compete against the champs. It's a matter of pride, a chance to prove that a player and a team can battle on even terms (and more) with the best.

So, while the 76ers were 65-17 in their championship season, they could only manage a record of 52-30 for their encore.

In any event, with Philadelphia's season terminated, up next for the Nets were the Milwaukee Bucks, who were paced by Sidney Moncrief, Marques Johnson, Junior Bridgeman, and Bob Lanier. Moncrief was a stopper and, as such, put a significant brake on Richardson's effectiveness, yet Otis Birdsong, Darryl Dawkins, Albert King, and Buck Williams picked up the slack, and every contest except game five (won by Milwaukee 94–82) was decided in the waning minutes. In the sixth and final game, and with no instant replay available, the referees counted a shot that Moncrief took after the buzzer that allowed the Bucks to close out the series with a 98–97 victory.

Hey, a righteous call would have extended the series to a decisive seventh game, where anything might have happened.

Despite the frustrating loss, everybody in the Nets organization was convinced that, with the sweetness returning to Sugar's game, the team would be a legitimate championship contender in 1984–85.

Playing It Straight . . . for a While

By the beginning of the 1984–85 season, Richardson had already burned through six agents, sixteen cars, a wife, and five rehab programs. Because he had repeatedly confessed to abusing drugs, only one negative "surprise" test counted against the NBA mandated limit of three strikes and you're out. Yet he was forced to stay straight by submitting to four or five drug tests every week. Undoubtedly, his being clean was why Richardson was also burning up opponents on the court.

Richardson wound up averaging a career-high 20.1 points per game, leading the NBA in steals for the third time, finishing in sixth place with 8.2 assists, participating in his fourth All-Star Game, and being chosen as the NBA's Comeback Player of the Year. Richardson's play was so overwhelming that most basketball pundits believed he was a much better player than the rookie Michael Jordan would ever be.

However, the Nets' hopes to be a serious championship contender were dashed when Otis Birdsong was in and out of the lineup due to a series of injuries, Albert King's leg miseries limited him to only forty-two games, and back problems shortened Darryl Dawkins's season to thirty-nine games.

There was every rational excuse for the Nets to limp through a 42-40 regular season and then get swept in three games by the Pistons. In fact Stan Albeck did a remarkable job keeping his diminished team competitive throughout. But shortly after the Detroit series, Albeck was fired.

Coaches get fired for various reasons: a revolt by the players (which was why Pat Riley was canned by the Lakers in 1990), a newly hired general manager who wants to hire a coach of his own, a coach might be too hard assed or too soft around the edges, or mostly for incompetence. Perhaps Joe Taub thought Albeck wasn't forceful enough, but he most likely was extremely disappointed when the Nets failed to live up to the lofty expectations raised by their defeating the defending champion Philadelphia 76ers in the 1984 playoffs. Never mind the rash of critical injuries. A step backward was simply unacceptable.

Besides, Albeck's public bristling at Taub's cancelling that postseason practice created a hostile vibration between them. In any event Albeck moved on to coach the Chicago Bulls to a disastrous 30-52 record in 1985–86, and he finished his NBA career as an assistant with several teams.

Albeck was replaced by Dave Wohl, a thirty-six-year-old former point guard who had concluded his ten-year active career with New Jersey in 1978. His reputation included an impressive basketball IQ, a highly serious demeanor, and an overriding ambition.

As such, Wohl demanded total discipline and totally lost his cool whenever that discipline was breached. If Richardson's habitual light-hearted approach to the game infuriated Wohl, the Nets new coach was even more upset with the antics of Chocolate Thunder.

For example, here's what occurred before one practice session early in the season: The players were lying on their backs on the court as the trainer led them through various warm-up exercises. The arena was silent except for the trainer's occasional directions. Meanwhile Wohl strode through the ranks of the sprawled players wearing a neatly pressed team sweat suit and an air of propriety.

Suddenly the earnest silence was ruptured by a shrill falsetto voice: "Oh, Old Black Joe! Could y'all sing for me one of them Nee-gra spirituals y'all sing so well?"

The faux question was answered with a lazy, sonorous baritone: "Yas'm, Missy Viola. I'se sure be delighted to sing for y'all."

It was Dawkins, of course, who then broke into song: "Ole man ribber, dat ole man ribber . . ."

Wohl was instantly apoplectic. "Let's get serious here, Darryl! Practice is no time to be fooling around!"

But it was too late. Whatever decorum had previously been present was now destroyed as the players convulsed with laughter. Their laughter turned into hysteria when Dawkins responded to his coach's request in the same drowsy Ante Bellum tone: "Yah suh, Mistah Boss Man."

Wohl could barely contain his rage but, knowing there was nothing he could do at the moment, said nothing.

However, here's what Richardson said about Wohl: "He's another tight-assed motherfucker." As such, definitely not Micheal Ray's latest father figure.

Even so, with Birdsong, King, and Dawkins healthy; with the steady defense and board work of Buck Williams; with the return of the explosive albeit inconsistent scoring of Mickey Johnson via free agency; and with the emergence of Mike Gminski, the Nets got off to an impressive start.

But there was an ominous sign of things to come when, on November 10, Richardson missed a team flight to San Antonio. "Given his past history," said Wohl, "you have to be a little more concerned than you normally would be about someone else."

Richardson finally joined the team late the next day and issued two different excuses: First he claimed to have had "car trouble," then he confessed to having "personal family problems." There was no direct public mention of his absence being drug related.

In any event, the Nets were 19-12 when they gathered for that infamous Christmas party.

Even before Richardson vamoosed with the blonde, Darryl Dawkins knew that something was off. He had been convinced for some time that the only players under surveillance by the NBA were blacks. Sometimes a coach whispered to a black player that he was being followed. Sometimes a drug-using black player found a warning note in his locker. "But I've seen plenty of white guys coming to games with their noses running," says Dawkins. "In fact, there were a couple of white stars who used to sit on the bench with towels over their heads, and the talk among the players was that their noses would start bleeding whenever they sat down."

According to Dawkins, back in the '70s and '80s, there's no doubt that the NBA looked the other way even when presented with evidence that white players were using: "It was only when the black guys started making enough money to join the fun that the NBA started making antidrug rules. I talked to one white franchise player who was busted by the league and instructed to tell everybody that he was going to Europe in the off-season. Meanwhile, he spent the summer drying out in some private clinic, and the drug busts were never hung on him. The talk among the players was that if a guy was being promoted as part of the NBA's marketing program, the league couldn't afford to have him disgraced. There was also some talk that the same easy deal also went down for a couple of black future Hall of Famers, but when the average black player got busted he stayed busted."

Indeed, Richardson, himself, had shared a pipe or two with at least one of these privileged white players. Another widely believed undercover story that made the round among NBA players proposed that a certain white superstar had run over and killed somebody while driving in a drug fog—but a hefty payment to the victim's family kept the deed under wraps.

It's interesting to enumerate all of the NBA players (in addition to Richardson) who had previously run afoul of the league's drug policy and were fined and/or suspended and/or forced to enter a rehab program.

Lucious Allen—marijuana, 1972
Bernard King—marijuana, cocaine, alcohol, 1977, 1978, 1980
Eddie Johnson—cocaine, alcohol, 1980
John Lucas—cocaine, 1981, 1982, 1983, 1984
John Drew—cocaine, 1982, 1984
Quintin Daley—cocaine, 1983
David Thompson—cocaine, 1983
Marques Johnson—cocaine, 1983
Walter Davis—cocaine, 1985

In addition, on May 23, 1980, Terry Furlow was killed in a one-car accident with alcohol and cocaine in his system.

Note that not a single white player is listed.

It was also standard practice for the NBA to try to deliberately lure players into using illicit drugs. When Dawkins was with the Utah Jazz, one of his teammates had just been released from a rehab program. The Jazz were on the road, when Dawkins got a 3:00 a.m. phone call from this player. "Hey, man," the player said, "I got a joint down here, but there's no matches in the room. Why don't you bring some matches with you and we'll do up this doobie?"

Back then, hotels didn't have no-smoking rooms, and every hotel room in the country came equipped with matches. Dawkins refused, and says, "It wouldn't have been the first or last time that a player on the edge was persuaded to set up a teammate."

Lewis Lloyd and Mitchell Wiggins were teammates on the 1985–86 Houston Rockets. After one home game, Lloyd and Wiggins went to a local nightclub to relax. Another Rockets player, Robert Reid, testified as to what happened then: "They were leaving the club, and this guy came up to them and told them, 'Hey, man, I've got something outside. This is good shit. It's the best. Just take a little bump.' And they told me, they took a little bump. The next day, [the NBA security chief] Horace Balmer and them were at practice. They were there at nine a.m. when we started practice. You cannot leave New York City in the morning to be in Houston that early the same morning. So you would have to be there the night before. I knew then that Lewis and Mitchell got set up."

Lloyd agreed: "We were definitely set up. Probably somebody on our team arranged it."

It was deemed essential, then, to have a black player be booted from the NBA after accruing a third strike. Hopefully, this would scare the white hoopers straight. And Richardson was an obvious target.

Even though Richardson remains convinced that the blonde with whom he absconded was merely an innocent civilian, a woman who couldn't resist his charms, many of his teammates believed that he had also been set up. After all, it was common knowledge around the league that Walter Davis was forced into a rehab program when he took an undercover female drug agent hired by the NBA up to his room to do a couple of lines.

And Dawkins is totally convinced that Richardson's Christmas party disaster was another set up: "Early in the '83–'84 season, Sugar and I were at a party at some girl's house after a ball game in Boston. Sugar went into a back room with one of the girls and was gone for over an hour. I was getting ready to head back to the hotel, so I asked some guy to go tell Sugar that it was time to leave. So the guy came back saying that Sugar and the girl had ducked out the back way and were gone. The guy said that the girl was definitely taking Sugar to some place where they could score some coke, and he knew exactly where that was. So we called for a cab and were suspicious when it showed up. The driver was a black guy, clean-shaven, nice hair, dressed in an expensive suit and tie, and he was driving very cautiously like he didn't know his way around the city. We found Sugar and got him back to the house, but another hour later him and the girl were gone again. I had to get back to the hotel, so we called for another cab. When the cab arrived, it was the same cab and the same driver as before. After a few blocks, the driver pulled over to the curb. Then he slid back the glass partition and said, 'Where the fuck is Micheal Ray?'

"'I don't know.'

"'When you see him, tell him we're gonna get him. It's only a question of when and where.'

"When he dropped me off at the hotel, he just drove away without asking me for a dime."

Richardson brushed off Dawkins's warning. "They ain't real c-cops or nothing. It ain't a problem, b-believe me."

Meanwhile, in December 1985, immediately upon returning to the team after his three-day postparty drug-and-sex idyll, Richardson met with Lew Schafel, the Nets general manager, and made a full confession. His subsequent drug test was positive, a result which nailed him with strike two. While the NBA pondered how to react to Richardson's latest drug episode, he was allowed to check into a rehab facility in Van Nuys, California.

While Richardson was rehabbing, the Nets regressed from sporting the third-best record in the Eastern Conference to the sixth slot. Also, with Dawkins still recovering from his back miseries and only able to play periodically, the team missed the fun-loving antics of their two most gregarious individuals. Indeed, sans Dawkins and Richardson, Wohl's hard-edged personality was unmitigated, and the players were increasingly on edge.

Following one particularly frustrating loss, a heated post-game locker-room shouting match between Mickey Johnson and Mike Gminski resulted in the former smashing his fist through a blackboard. The reason for their confrontation was their differing opinions of Richardson.

"I'm going to miss him from head to foot," said Johnson. "We had a strong relationship. The fire, the unpredictability, the fact that he was never afraid."

"Professionally," said Gminski, "Micheal Ray had a direct negative effect on my livelihood. But as a human being, you don't want to see him fail either. He may not be your favorite person, but you want to see him beat it. So, you're caught halfway."

Buck Williams took a much broader view: "Maybe a kid in Connecticut or a kid in Brooklyn who might be thinking about drugs will take a look at Micheal Ray Richardson and think twice about it."

After his three-week stint in his latest rehab clinic, Richardson was "squeaky clean." On January 20, 1986, a press conference was convened to announce his reinstatement to the Nets roster. He began by saying somewhat disingenuously that he couldn't remember the details that led to his suspension but that he understood that he had "a disease" and was angry at himself for what he had done. He also apologized to his teammates and to the fans, yet didn't expect any of them to fully understand the manifestations of his disease. He concluded by saying this: "Maybe I didn't like myself for some of the things I have done, but deep down I love myself."

The Nets had gone 6-5 in his absence, with Darwin Cook filling in admirably at the point-guard position. And the two Nets who were interviewed, welcomed Richardson back into the fold.

"Everything is back to normal," said Buck Williams. "The vibes are good."

"We've been through this before," said Otis Birdsong. "You can't hold a grudge or have any animosity toward him. He's one of a million people who are trying to deal with this problem. He needs our support, and we need him to accomplish our goal, which is to win an NBA championship."

As part of the reinstatement agreement, the Nets then arranged for a local psychiatrist, Dr. Russell Ferstandig, to conduct Richardson's outpatient program. Micheal Ray was absolutely enthusiastic: "Great. The shrink was going to help me stay straight. Right?"

Yet despite Richardson's (and the Nets') optimistic expectations, his preliminary interview with Dr. Ferstandig was somewhat disturbing. "The first thing he does," says Micheal Ray, "is to give me a hundred bucks. Then he tells me to go into New York right away and buy the same stuff that I was using. He said he was going to test the drugs on himself in order to get a full understanding of what was going on. What the fuck? But if that's what he wanted, who was I to tell him no. So I went and got the drugs and brought them back to him."

As long as he was buying drugs again, Richardson decided he might as well get some for himself. This led to his using on a regular basis once more. (And which eventually resulted in Richardson's filing a malpractice suit against Ferstandig.)

Richardson was totally surprised when he reported for their first official session the next morning. "The guy was sitting in his chair, wearing the same clothes as the day before, and stoned out like a zombie. Un-fucking-believable. Even so, I was anxious to stay with the program, so we did our fucked-up therapy sessions a few times. Then, two weeks later, Ferstandig got busted buying drugs in Greenwich Village."

Next up, Schafel produced another psychiatrist in the area. "But it was already too late," says Richardson, "because, even after I returned to the Nets, I started dipping and dabbing again. This new guy, Dr. X, didn't help matters when he agreed to hide my positive drug tests for a fee of about two hundred dollars each."

But there was more Sturm und Drang to come.

There had been a mini-epidemic of flu and flu-like symptoms among NBA players, and on February 11, Richardson was suspended for one game for blowing off a scheduled visit to a doctor for a routine flu check up. Suspecting that drug abuse was behind Richardson's absence, the Nets subjected him to a drug test, which he passed.

Meanwhile, his second marriage was on the rocks. His wife, Leah, had obtained a court order barring Richardson from the house in Mahwah, New Jersey, that he owned and where she lived. A few days later—at 1:00 a.m. on the morning of February 20—he broke into the house and engaged in a furious argument with Leah, who promptly called the police and had Micheal Ray arrested. In his defense, Richardson claimed that he was unaware of the restraining order. Immediately after his release, the NBA mandated a drug test which Richardson failed.

This latest result constituted strike three and meant a "permanent" banishment from the NBA, with the only out being the opportunity to petition the league for reinstatement after two years. Since reinstatement was highly unlikely, both the media and the players called the punishment "The Death Sentence."

Even though Richardson stoutly denied taking any drugs, his agent, Charles Grantham, decided not to appeal the judgment.

Micheal Ray's final NBA season lasted for forty-seven games and produced 15.7 points, 7.2 assists, and 2.66 steals per game. The shock and distractions he created left the Nets with a gravely disappointing record of 39-43.

In making the official announcement, David Stern rued the extreme but necessary punishment: "This is a tragic day for Micheal Ray Richardson. Nothing less than the destruction by cocaine of a once-flourishing career." That Stern felt compassion for Richardson would be demonstrated several times in the coming years.

A funereal tone overwhelmed Richardson's (now) former team-mates. "Banned for life," said Buck Williams. "That sounds like cancer . . . he has no hope." Williams added that Richardson had an insatiable need "to be loved."

"It was like Micheal Ray has died," said Otis Birdsong.

"To be honest," one player said, "I figured it would happen sooner or later."

Schaffel noted that the Nets organization gave Richardson total "support and guidance" and even paid for his rehabilitation costs.

Larry Doby, the Nets' director of community relations, had the most incisive comment: "Micheal Ray Richardson is not a problem child. He is a child with a problem."

Indeed, the all-too-common truth is that playing basketball on a professional level tends to prolong a player's adolescence. Virtually all of them have been recruited and coddled since they were teenagers. As a result, they routinely lack even a minimal sense of being responsible for their own lives. Agents negotiate their contracts, handle their income-tax returns, pay their credit-card bills, and often put tens of thousands of dollars aside to pay for abortions. Accordingly, too many players never write checks, do not know how to balance a checkbook, and rely on flunkies to stock their refrigerators and buy their toilet paper.

Others around the league were not at all sympathetic. "I'm glad the NBA wrote it strong," said Jerry Krause, the Chicago Bulls' general manager. "Richardson made his own bed, and now he has to sleep in it."

Stan Albeck wasn't surprised: "[Professional basketball players] are emotionally very high-strung. They never have time to relax, and that turns them into walking time bombs. You hope for the best, but how can you have sympathy for someone who broke the rules three times? How many chances does a normal guy get to break the law?"

It should be noted that just one month before Richardson's banishment, John Drew received the same sentence but under different and far more serious circumstances. Drew, a former All-Star with Atlanta who was then with the Utah Jazz, had been arrested twice in less than three months, once for selling cocaine to an undercover police officer and then for trying to buy cocaine from a similar source. At the time of Richardson's downfall, Drew was playing with the Wyoming Wildcatters in the minor-league Continental Basketball Association.

But, in the immediate aftermath of his suspension, Richardson was in no mood to play basketball.

"Getting kicked out of the NBA was the lowest point of my life," said Richardson. "I was a punk-ass kid from nowhere, so the NBA thought I was expendable. There's a double-standard in the league. Believe me, when I got kicked out, all of them white druggies threw away their pipes and got clean in a hurry. The NBA got exactly what they wanted. There's no question in my mind that there was a double standard."

Richardson's charge of institutional racism in the NBA coincided with the league's long history of discrimination (and worse) against black players.

While Chuck Cooper was the first black player drafted by an NBA team—the Boston Celtics in April 1950—Earl Lloyd was the first black to actually play in an NBA game—with the Washington Capitals versus the Rochester Royals on October 31, 1950.

However, on November 7, 1902, Harry "Bucky" Lew was paid five dollars by the Pawtucket Athletic Club for playing against a team from the town of Marlborough, Massachusetts, in the New England Basketball League—thereby qualifying as the first black pro. More than a decade later, the Harlem Rens (formed in 1923) and the Harlem Globetrotters (1927) were highly successful all-black touring teams. A handful of black players participated in several other transient pro leagues until 1942, when the Chicago Studebaker Champions competed in the National Basketball League with a roster that featured four white and six black players.

For sure, while Cooper and Lloyd did not experience the same level of racial abuse as Jackie Robinson did when he joined the Brooklyn Dodgers in 1947, they were not immune to some race baiting. When the Celtics visited the Milwaukee Hawks on February 2, 1952, one of the home team's players twice called Cooper a "Black bastard." After Cooper retaliated with a forceful shove, the offending player backed away and refused to fight. However, an extended melee did occur, including some fisticuffs between Boston's coach, Red Auerbach, and his opposite number, Doxie Moore.

Years later, the legendary Oscar Robertson was not surprised by the incident. During his career in Milwaukee (1970–74), the Big O was convinced that the city was essentially a racist one.

Cooper was not allowed to play in an exhibition game that pitted the Celtics against the Milwaukee Hawks in Baton Rouge, Louisiana. All of the Hawks came over to Boston's bench to express their disapproval of the city's Jim Crow law by shaking Cooper's hand. All, that is, except Bob Pettit, who had been born and raised in Baton Rouge.

Nor was Pettit's native racism confined to this gesture. During the 1961–62 season, the Hawks had relocated to St. Louis and had drafted a dynamic black player, Cleo Hill, from Winston-Salem State. Pettit, along with fellow southerner Cliff Hagan, took umbrage at Hill's presence, who joined the little-used Lenny Wilkens as being the only blacks on the team. Accordingly, Pettit and Hagan refused to pass to the six-foot-one Hill, complained that he shot too much, and lobbied coach Paul Seymour to keep him glued to the bench. Seymour, however, greatly valued Hill's explosive scoring and threatened to fine Pettit and Hagan, and even to physically assault them, but to no avail. Ben Kerner owned the Hawks and his solution was to fire Seymour and replace him with Fuzzy Levane. It's worth noting that under Seymour, Hill's per game averages included 28 minutes, 10.8 points, and 5.5 rebounds, while under Levane his numbers decreased to 15 minutes, 4.1 points, and 2.4 rebounds.

Hill was waived after the season and never played another game in the NBA.

In general, blacks were only allowed to do dirty work—defend and rebound. Elgin Baylor, drafted in the first round by the Minneapolis Lakers in 1958, was the first black player with a carte blanche license to shoot.

Earl Lloyd also reported that rather than call a foul on a white player, refs routinely called fouls on him even when he wasn't anywhere in the vicinity of the play.

In 1948 Don Barksdale was the first black on a U.S. Olympic basketball team. Five years later, he became the first black to play in an NBA All-Star Game. According to him, NBA coaches took pains to insure that, whenever possible, black players only guarded each other. Cooper and Barksdale, Nat Clifton and Lloyd are the examples Barksdale gave.

And, of course, it was no secret that for many years NBA rosters had an unofficial quota of black players. Calvin Ramsey was a six-foot-four, two-hundred-pound rebounding machine from NYU who played in a total of thirteen games for St. Louis, New York, and Syracuse during the 1959–60 and 1960–61 seasons. "It was the same thing with all of those teams," says Ramsey. "I was tearing it up every time I came off the bench, but there were four blacks on each of those teams and one of us had to go. That one was me."

The three-blacks-per-team quota gradually increased through the late '60s—mainly because Red Auerbach began starting three, then four, and then five black players. However, many of even the most loyal Celtic fans were distressed at Auerbach's racially blind tactics.

Although the suffocating defense of Bill Russell was the primary reason why the Celtics won eleven championships during his thirteen seasons (1956–69) in Boston, on several occasions intruders broke into his home and defecated on his bed. Indeed, Russell once had the following conversation with George Sullivan, a sportswriter for the *Boston Herald Traveler*:

"Boston," said Russell, "is the most racist city in the United States."

"Say that one more time," said Sullivan, "and I'll write it."

After repeating his accusation, Russell added, "Your paper doesn't have the guts to run that story."

And Russell was correct.

In the late 1960s, the upstart American Basketball Association was raiding NBA rosters, signing as many of the established league's top stars as money could buy. Golden State's Rick Barry had led the NBA in scoring during the 1966–67 campaign with a remarkable points-per-game average of 35.6, but in the subsequent off-season, he signed with the ABA's Oakland Oaks. There was a sense of consternation among the NBA's bigwigs and a half-hearted lawsuit was instituted by Golden State to regain the rights to Barry, but the general attitude was that business was business. Indeed, five years later Barry was welcomed back into the NBA with open arms.

Joe Caldwell, an All-Star guard with the Atlanta Hawks, similarly jumped to the ABA in 1970. But when the ABA and NBA merged in 1976, not only was Caldwell forbidden to return to NBA action, but several guarantees in his ABA contract were illegally ignored. As a result, Caldwell was deprived of nearly a million dollars, and his litigation has been dragging through the courts ever since.

The difference between Barry and Caldwell? The former, of course, is white, while the latter is black.

In the early spring of 1971, Earl Monroe was the Baltimore Bullets leading scorer. A certified All-Star with dazzling moves, Monroe believed that, on the court and off, he was "the team leader." While a student at Winston-Salem State, he "became more and more aware of how black people were being treated in this country." That's when he started wearing red/black/green headbands and hats—a color combination that represented the liberation of Africans as well as African Americans. Otherwise, Monroe kept his commitment to the civil rights movement to himself.

However, even though he characterizes Baltimore as "basically a southern city," and even though what he calls his "red/black/green experience" didn't meet with universal approval, "I loved the city," he says, "and most everybody loved me."

That is, until he happened to be on hand for a high-school basketball game between a white team and a black team. The competition was fierce, and before long, students from the two schools were engaged in a confrontation that was sufficiently violent for the local police to be called to the scene. From where he sat, Monroe could see that the white cops were focused on beating up the black kids—so he rushed on to the court to try to calm the situation. Despite his fair-minded and peaceful intentions, Monroe was quickly arrested.

When both the Bullets' front office and the NBA publicity machine made him out to be a Black Power sympathizer and all-around troublemaker, Monroe deduced that "the NBA was itching to throw me out of the league."

After a summer's worth of negative publicity, Monroe forced the Bullets to trade him. Indeed, after appearing in the Bullets first three games in the following season, he was dealt to the Knicks. "I definitely thought," he recalls, "that playing with the Knicks would be my last chance to get straight with the basketball establishment before I was booted out of the NBA."

Just a year later, Roy Rubin was coaching the woefully inept Philadelphia 76ers (who finished the season with a record of 9-73) when the 1973 All-Star Game was nigh. Two weeks before the event it was announced that the 76ers' representative would be John Block. "That's remarkable," said Block. "The highlight of this lousy season." Most of Block's teammates, however, were outraged.

"Back then," says one member of the team who requested anonymity, "the coaches picked the All-Star players. The selection rules were that every team had to be represented and that the coaches could not vote for any of their own players. Well, the word got back to us that Rubin had been calling all the other coaches and telling them to vote for Block. The obvious and righteous choice would have been Freddie Carter. That was a no-brainer. Carter was the team's leading scorer and assist man, plus he rebounded like a big man. There was no question in our minds that Rubin had successfully lobbied for the white guy over the black guy. No doubt at all."

There has always been a certain disdain that black players have historically had for their white counterparts. One example that proves the point is Pete Maravich, a scoring machine whose flashy game was disrespected by virtually all of the NBA's black players. Here's what Wali Jones had to say about Pistol Pete: "He made a career out of copying what black players have always been doing. But he's white and it's a white media and that's where the ink is and the bread is. That cat's a good ballplayer, but he's too studied. He can't make those unknown moves that a guy like Earl Monroe can. Underneath the mechanics, Maravich is still straight up-and-down."

Then there was Isaiah Thomas, who opined that Larry Bird wouldn't have been so universally celebrated if he was black.

Also, less than a year after the 2004 "Malice in the Palace" disgrace, David Stern implemented a strict dress code. Whenever players were arriving at a game or engaged in any activity on behalf of the NBA, they had to wear business attire—dress shoes, slacks with jackets or suits, and neckties. Hats, baggy jeans, T-shirts, sneakers, Timberland boots, and any other gear associated with hip-hop culture were forbidden and would subject the guilty players to large fines. Plus, unless they were riding on team buses or chartered airplanes, or safely inside locker rooms, players were forbidden to wear headphones, visible chains, or sleeveless shirts.

At the time, Jason Richardson was a standout guard with the Golden State Warriors, and he was displeased with Stern's edicts: "One thing to me that was kind of racist was you can't wear chains outside your clothing. I don't understand what that has to do with being business approachable. You wear a suit, you still could be a crook."

David J. Leonard addressed the issue in his book *After Artest: The NBA and the Assault on Blackness*. Stern's ruling "would come to embody the NBA's most systematic effort to alter its image in order to bring back its red state fans and corporate sponsors. According to an NBA official, the dress code was designed to appease corporate anxieties about the league's hip-hop image and protect the NBA's economic future."

During Stern's tenure as NBA commissioner, the league experienced four lockouts and a collective-bargaining process that rendered the players' union one of the weakest in professional sports. Boyce Watkins observed, "Stern fully understands is that it's easier to be a capitalist overseer when controlling black men than for any other group of people."

The comments of Bryant Gumbel, on an episode of HBO's *Real Sports*, were even more pointed: "[Stern] has always seemed eager to be viewed as some kind of modern plantation owner treating NBA men as if they were his boys."

Moreover, despite the 2008 election of Barack Obama, the Supreme Court's rulings on affirmative action and voting rights demonstrate that America is far from being a post-racial society. As far as the NBA is concerned, the most current (and most publicized) indications that racism remains alive and unwell are the 2014 case of Donald Sterling, the one-time owner of the Los Angeles Clippers, as well as that of Bruce Levenson, who possessed controlling interest in the Atlanta Hawks, and the Hawks' general manager Danny Ferry.

For sure, Sterling deserved his expulsion from the NBA and his $2.5 million fine for his racist rants, but for years (nay, decades) the league's bigwigs pointedly ignored clear evidence of Sterling's anti-black views. The most significant of these was a lawsuit brought in federal courts by several African American and Latino tenants in Sterling's numerous rental properties in Los Angeles. Their suit alleged that Sterling expressed a racial bias in declining to make sorely needed repairs in these buildings. Among the charges leveled against Sterling was his saying that "black tenants smell and attract vermin." Although Sterling never admitted any wrongdoing, he did negotiate a $2.5 million settlement with his accusers.

Then there was an airport meeting with Rollie Massimino back in 1983 when Sterling was interviewing possible replacements for the recently fired Paul Silas. In his role as the Clippers general manger, Paul Phipps was also present at the meeting. According to Phipps, one of Sterling's questions to Massimino was this: "I wanna know why you think you can coach these niggers."

There were many other reports of Sterling's making racially charged comments about various black celebrities ranging from Beyoncé to Charles Barkley.

Even so, through the years while the NBA was fining Dallas Mavericks owner Mark Cuban over $2 million for his public criticisms of the league's referees, and while the Knicks' J. R. Smith was fined $25,000 for reaching down and untying an opponent's shoelaces during a free throw, Sterling was never warned, castigated, or fined for his blatant antiblack comments.

Before the Sterling tapes were made public—and in a league where roughly 80 percent of the players were black—racism in the owners' mansions and penthouses was routinely ignored. In fact the NBA brain trust was more concerned with the reaction to Sterling's words than to the content. With the Clippers' coach, Doc Rivers, suggesting that fans boycott the team's games and the players threatening to follow suit, and with team and league sponsors also on the verge of withdrawing their support, the NBA's board of governors had no choice but to punish Sterling to the max.

Barely a year later, Levenson was quoted as saying that the presence of too many blacks at the Hawks' games "scared away the whites and there are simply not enough affluent black fans to build a significant season base." Levenson also complained that too many of the Hawks' cheerleaders were black and that the hip-hop music played for their dance routines was specifically aimed at a black audience.

When these comments became public, Levenson was forced to sell his stake in the team.

Danny Ferry's miscue was to read a scouting report on Luol Deng during an in-house conference call. According to the report, Deng was a "good guy," but "he's got some African in him." Ferry then compared Deng to someone who had "a nice store out front but sells counterfeit stuff out the back."

For this transgression, Ferry was compelled to take an unpaid, indefinite leave of absence.

Meanwhile, there were probably several executives of other franchises who had some emails and voice mails erased.

Another case in point was Golden State's sudden firing of coach Mark Jackson after he had led the 2013–14 Warriors to fifty-two wins. Almost simultaneously, the Warriors announced that Jackson's replacement would be Steve Kerr. It should be remembered that back in the 1960s, Oakland was the birthplace of the Black Panthers and remains the most racially charged city in the country. So it's not surprising that one of the Warriors' black players was suspicious about an experienced black coach getting canned in favor of a white man who had never coached basketball at any level.

"We had to look at it," said the player, "from a racial standpoint."

Kerr, of course, validated his hiring by leading the Warriors to the NBA championship in 2015.

Who, then, could disagree that Richardson's bitter complaints about what he identified as the NBA's "double standard" was more than merely a case of sour grapes? In any event, Richardson's expulsion from the league was a painful disaster, a disaster of his own making, but a disaster nevertheless. "The only response I was capable of," he recalls, "was to go off on a week-long binge. I stayed in a hotel room in New York with six women, and we had a nonstop drug orgy."

Meanwhile, there were piles of unpaid bills and mortgage payments, so Richardson set about to pick up his last check from the Nets. Not wanting to face anybody from the organization, he entered the Meadowlands Arena through a back door and had a low-level Nets employee bring the check to him.

"When I finally came to my senses," Richardson recalls, "I realized that I'd lost my career and was lucky I hadn't lost my life. What did I have left? Not my self-respect. Not any hope that some counselor or rehab program could straighten me out. Not any kind of spiritual belief. Not a strong male figure who could tell me what to do. Even my momma was disgusted with me. All I had was some money—about $250,000. But that wouldn't last long if I continued hitting the pipe."

Life after Death

On June 17, 1986, the Boston Celtics gleefully used their second overall pick in the college draft to select Len Bias, a six-foot-eight, 210-pound forward from Maryland who was advertised as the second coming of Michael Jordan. Bias would be the franchise player who would lead the Celtics back to the Russellian glory days of the mid-1950s to the late '60s.

Two days later, Bias was dead of a cocaine overdose.

It was a grievous tragedy for the young man and his family, a setback for the future hopes of the Celtics, and another grim reminder that cocaine continued to be a huge problem for the NBA.

Barely two weeks later, Richardson ignored the same restraining order that ultimately had resulted in his banishment from the NBA by once more pounding on the front door of his wife's house. After being spotted by the police, he escaped into some adjacent woods. That afternoon he was found sleeping in his wife's Mercedes-Benz convertible—with the motor running—behind a real-estate office in nearby Allendale. When his wife, Leah, came to the police station to sign a complaint, Richardson threatened her verbally and physically.

In the opinion of Frank Parenti, Allendale's police chief, "He was on something. He's a very sick boy. He's thin, his face was drawn, and he looks terrible."

Richardson was booked for assault and driving with a revoked license. His date in court was set for August 26, and his bail of $2,500 was posted by his current girlfriend, Brenda Dyla.

After this latest incident, Richardson had an epiphany. "It finally came to me that all I had left was my love for the game of basketball," he said. "Period. So that's where I started from."

When a pay-for-play team in Israel expressed an interest in Richardson, his wife rescinded her complaint, and at her prompting, an Allendale judge likewise agreed to drop all criminal charges against Micheal Ray. This marked the beginning of reconciliation between Richardson and Leah. Accordingly, on October 28, 1986, Richardson was permitted to sign a $60,000 contract to play with Hapoel Ramat Gan, a declining team that was desperate to compete against the reigning Israeli champions, Maccabi Tel Aviv. Avraham Hemo was the coach and manager of Hapoel, and as an ex-police officer he believed that Richardson could restart his career under his tight supervision.

At the time, the level of competition in Israel was mediocre at best and poor at worst. Neal Walk was a six-foot-ten center who had played in the NBA for eight years—with Phoenix, New Orleans, and New York. While with the Suns in the 1972–73 season, he had averaged 20.2 points, 12.4 rebounds, and 3.5 assists per game. Where he once was a banger, Walk had become a vegetarian, shed 30 pounds, and, weighing 220, had transformed into a finesse player. After his NBA career ended in 1977, Walk played several productive seasons in Italy before taking his game to Israel from 1983 to 1984.

"I enjoyed the people," Walk says, "the history, and the always willing sabra women. But the level of play was pretty bad. To keep myself from getting bored, I concentrated on passing and rebounding. The only shots I looked to take were bank shots with my off hand. Even so, I soon lost interest, and my competitive chops atrophied to the point where, when I returned to the States and tried to make a comeback with the Utah Jazz, I had forgotten how to play at an NBA level and was cut early in training camp."

At first, Richardson had several reasons to like being in Israel. "Despite the suicide bombings and other stuff," said Richardson, "I wasn't afraid coming to Israel because I had visited the country before when the Nets played some exhibition games there. All I wanted was a chance to keep on playing basketball."

Once there, Richardson was impressed by the spirit of the Israelis, their food, the "beautiful women," and the grand opening of the Cinerama, "a wild club." He was also impressed with the Israeli's appreciation of James Brown, whom Richardson saw as presenting the collective spirit of his own people. Perhaps, Micheal Ray, thought, the Israelis might also embrace him.

If Richardson was not afraid to go to Israel, several important politicians were ostensibly afraid of him. Micha Reiser, a Kneset member of the conservative Likud party, objected to "a drug-addicted American player" coming to Israel. His objection was seconded by Pinhas Goldstein, the head of the country's sport and education committee, who attacked Richardson as being a "non-educational figure." The specter of Richardson's playing with Hopoel was deemed by Miki Berkovic, the star of Maccabia Tel Aviv, as "a shameful disgrace."

On February 25, 1967, the Munich-based Federation of International Basketball Association (FIBA), the sport's governing body, refused to approve Richardson's contract with Hapoel. The unspoken reason given, of course, was his history of drug abuse, but the official motivation for the ban was "there was no official document indicating that Richardson was released from an amateur team that he used to play for in Denver."

Whatever that meant.

"The real reason," said Richardson, "was that Maccabia Tel Aviv had a strong connection with FIBA and were worried that my playing with Hapoel would be a serious challenge to their dominance. And they had good reason to be afraid of me because if I had played with Hapoel, I believe we would have beaten Maccabia and taken the championship from them."

Despite the FIBA's bogus decision and the widespread public slander, Richardson remained in Israel, hoping that somehow the ruling would be overturned. In lieu of playing, Richardson became Avraham Hemo's assistant coach, but his initial experience on the bench was frustrating. "The players were always bitching and screaming."

After the six-month Israeli season ended, Richardson returned home and focused on repairing his relationship with Leah. "She was very upset with me," he said, "which is only human. But she also loved me, and cared about me. I guess it's because she knows what kind of person I am when I'm not doing drugs."

Come spring, Richardson looked for another chance to play pro ball, this time in the States—and he had an extensive alphabet of minor leagues to choose from:

ACPBL—Atlantic Coast Professional Basketball League
CBA—Continental Basketball Association
CPBL—Canadian Professional Basketball League
EBL—Eastern Basketball Alliance
GBA—Global Basketball League
IBA—Independent Basketball Association
IBEL—Iowa Basketball Exposure League
IBL—International Basketball League
KBDL—Kentucky Basketball Developmental League
MEBL—Metro-East Basketball League
NABL—National Athletic Basketball League
NRL—National Rookie League

TRBL—Tobacco Road Basketball League
USBL—United States Basketball League
WBK—World Basketball League
WCPBL—West Coast Professional Basketball League

The most comparatively stable of these shaky organizations was the United States Basketball League (USBL) and the Continental Basketball Association (CBA). The USBL was the brainchild of a venture capitalist named Daniel Meisenheimer III, who in 1985 envisioned a league that played from May to July, stretched from coast to coast, and would eventually be a farm system for NBA ballclubs. His dream included fifty teams grouped in eight divisions with players' salaries ranging from $300 to $1,000 per week. Joining Meisenheimer at the press conference announcing the USBL's formation were Walt Frazier and Dick Barnett, who were introduced as the franchise owners in Atlanta and White Plains, New York. Also on hand was Earl Monroe, slated to be the USBL's first commissioner. When that initial season commenced, neither Frazier nor Barnett were involved. Monroe was soon replaced by Meisenheimer himself, and only seven franchises answered the opening bell. Altogether, these charter franchises lost a total of $1.2 million

By the time Richardson signed with the Long Island Knights, the eight surviving teams had each previously played a thirty-game season, but the USBL continued to be strictly a fly-by-night organization. During its twenty-two-year lifespan (1985–2007), the USBL featured teams in fifty-six cities—from Atlantic City to Dodge City, from Hoboken to Brooklyn—with none of them ever showing a profit. Indeed, the combination of shaky ownership, in-and-out franchises, and tiny crowds forced the league to cancel its 1989 season. Year by year, the lineup of teams dramatically shrank so that in the league's final two seasons, all of the surviving franchises were situated in Kansas, Nebraska, and Oklahoma.

Not even the appearance of several washed-up former NBA players—most notable among these were World B. Free, Manute Bol, and Spud Webb—could ever make the USBL a viable operation. The impossibility of any one team developing a loyal corps of fans was demonstrated during the 2000 season, when the USBL's eleven ballclubs combined to execute more than 200 trades involving 450 players.

One particular player did, however, generate considerable publicity for the USBL. This was Nancy Lieberman who joined Springfield Fame in 1986. The first woman to play in a men's pro league, Lieberman had been a member of the gold-medal-winning U.S. Olympic women's team in 1976 and was still considered to be the best female hooper in the known world. However, Lady Magic's on-court impact was minimal as she averaged a mere two points in twenty-one games. Moreover, despite the media hype the league-wide attendance was just over 825 per game.

Several of the USBL's coaches, though, would eventually graduate into NBA employment. Eric Musselman, for example, moved from the USBL to coach the Golden State Warriors and then the Sacramento Kings. Another NBA-bound coach was Henry Bibby, who despite a somewhat checkered past ultimately became a valuable assistant coach with several NBA teams.

Indeed, in Bibby's previous incarnation as coach of the CBA's Tulsa Zone, he was solely responsible for having the finest hotel in Albany, New York, close its doors to any and all CBA teams. This happened as a result of Bibby's propositioning his waitress in the Albany Hilton's restaurant, not knowing that she was the daughter of the city's archbishop. In fact, Bibby used to brag about his routine come-ons: "If I ask ten women to sleep with me, or twenty or more, one of them is bound to agree."

But womanizing wasn't Bibby's only in-season recreation: Like the NBA, the CBA conducted random pregame drug tests with certain players and coaches chosen by lot and letting the two coaches decide which one of them would be tested. Prior to one unexpected drug test, Bibby had begged a rival coach (which happened to be me!) to volunteer, citing his participation in a free-for-all party the night before. It was only fitting then that Bibby was destined to become one of Micheal Ray's USBL coaches.

Richardson's first team, the Long Island Knights, was coached by an ex-Knick, Dean Meminger. This was Dean the Dream's second coaching gig, the first being with the CBA's Albany Patroons in that team's inaugural season of 1982–83. At the time, Meminger was only thirty-four years old and five years removed from his last NBA campaign. During the Patroons' practices and games, Meminger would constantly ridicule his players, claiming that he was still better than any of them. But, after the Patroons began the season with a dismal record of 8-15, Meminger was fired. His temporary replacement was one of the players, Sam Worthen, who led the team to a pair of losses before a more permanent coach was hired.

Enter Phil Jackson, who had recently retired as a player and assistant coach with the New Jersey Nets and had retreated to his home in Montana where he was operating a local health club.

Before Meminger left town, he made a last request to be allowed to try out for the team. Phil agreed and watched a painful scrimmage wherein the surviving players unmercifully beat on their ex-coach.

Jackson finished the season at 8-11 and won the CBA championship in 1983–84. After three more seasons in the CBA, Jackson moved on to Chicago, Los Angeles, and the Hall of Fame.

Meanwhile, Richardson was happy to be making $10,000 for the short USBL season and was even happier to routinely pass the twice-a-week urinalysis monitored by a private addiction treatment center in New York. "Playing in this league is something I have to do," he said, "so I just go out and do it. This experience will serve its purpose for me." He also believed that once his two-year suspension was over, some NBA team would give him another opportunity to play in what the players called "The League." "If you can play, somebody will take a chance." And, indeed, he could still play, averaging 28 points, 9 rebounds, and 6 assists for the Knights and drawing raves from opposing players and coaches.

But no praise came from Meminger, who objected to Richardson's taking too many shots and habitually aborting the team's offensive patterns to freelance. On June 16 the Knights released Richardson, charging that he was disruptive to the team and disrespectful to Meminger. Richardson responded by claiming that the Knights bounced paychecks and ran an unprofessional organization. (Meminger died in 2013, having fought a losing battle with hard drugs.)

Two days later, Richardson was signed by the Jersey Jammers and Henry Bibby was his latest coach. After two weeks, Bibby said this about his new player: "I'm happy with his attitude. Wherever he goes in the NBA, he'll have to fit into a structured system. He has shown me he's trying to do that here."

Indeed, "structure" was, and is, the name of the game in the NBA.

There are two categories of offense: read offense and execution offense. The former is based on the principle that the defense cannot deny possession to the four players who do not have the ball. Trying to overplay all four invariably leads to backdoor cuts, lob passes, and uncontested layups. So, a read offense begins with a pass to whichever player is in position to receive a pass. This offense requires savvy players, impeccable coordination, total unselfishness, and stable rosters—situations which are simply not available to minor-league teams. The triangle offense designed by Phil Jackson and Tex Winter is the classic, and most successful, manifestation of a read offense.

In an execution offense, players have assigned routes in conjunction with each other—picks, curls, pops, fades, basket cuts, reversal passes—all within a certain structure. This might be a one-two-two alignment, or a one-three-one, etcetera. The goals here are many: to take advantage of lopsided mismatches, to create sufficient space for a player to take his opponent one on one so that double teaming by the defense becomes risky, to get the ball to a specific player in his most effective spots, to maintain sufficient floor balance so as to have enough retreating manpower to defend against fast breaks—and, above all, to get good shots.

The trouble is that in minor-league basketball virtually every player (rightly) believes that most NBA scouts are unduly impressed with individual statistics. So, the prevailing attitude on offense is to shoot first and never ask questions—which is why coaching at this level is so difficult and so frustrating. So, then, if Richardson's first two weeks under Bibby showed at least a modicum of self-control, Micheal Ray would inevitably be hard pressed to continue his acceptance of whatever structure that his latest coach demanded.

But as the season progressed, Richardson became disenchanted with the all-offense-no-defense game plans that most USBL teams employed, also with the cheap hotels, the lack of seriousness manifested by most of the other NBA veteran players, and the paltry crowds. "I'll be damned if I'm going to make this my career," he moaned. "I'm gonna put in my ten weeks, say thank you very much, and never see this again."

Despite Richardson's averaging 25.5 points, 7.3 assists, and 2.3 steals, the Jammers were 13-17 and losers in a one-game playoff appearance.

Back home in New Jersey, Micheal Ray and Leah effected a complete reconciliation even as he investigated his next move. If he wanted to stay in the States, Richardson decided that his only viable option was to follow the lead of John Drew and play in the Continental Basketball Association.

The first incarnation of the CBA occurred on April 23, 1946 (six weeks before the formation of the Basketball Association of America [BAA], the forerunner of the NBA), when the Eastern Professional Basketball League was chartered. Commonly called the "Eastern League" (EL), the six original franchises included the Wilkes-Barre Barons, the Lancaster Red Roses, the Reading Keys, the Allentown Rockets, the Hazelton Mountaineers, and the Pottsville Pros.

All of the franchises, and virtually all of the players, were located in Pennsylvania, and the best players earned $7,500 for the season—which was equivalent to the salaries paid by the established (but soon to be extinct) National Basketball League and the fledgling BAA.

The schedule wasn't balanced, with Lancaster playing thirty games, Allentown playing twenty-six, and the others either twenty-seven or twenty-eight. The games were played mostly on Saturday and Sunday nights, and players from out of town would usually travel with seven or eight guys packed into somebody's car. The teams played mostly in high-school and junior-high school gyms, and seven hundred fans were a big turnout. The officials were usually local high-school refs, and it was extremely rare for a team to win a game on the road.

For the next few years, the Eastern League played musical franchises with an increasing number of teams being sponsored by local businesses, such as the Berwick Carbuilders, the Lebanon Seltzers, and the Pottsville Packers. The rosters were still mainly populated with local heroes, including Philadelphians like Jack Ramsey and Jack McClosky, who both went on to be successful coaches in the NBA.

In 1948 the BAA merged with the National Basketball League to form the NBA, which reduced the total number of pro teams and likewise cut the available jobs. One result was that a number of elite players from New Jersey and New York were happy to earn anywhere from one hundred to three hundred dollars for a weekend's work with some Eastern League team of the moment.

Hubie Brown averaged 13.8 points while playing in eight games for the Rochester Zenith in the Eastern League's 1958–59 season. "Back then," Brown says, "there were only eight teams in the newly created NBA and only ten players on each team. That adds up to only eighty players. Guys played in the Eastern League because there was no place else for them to play, and it was a hell of a league. Everybody played a cerebral kind of game with a lot of motion. It was a form of passing game before anybody gave it a name. A lot of the old guys from the Northeast called it Jew basketball. I'm telling you the truth here, that many of the guys in the Eastern League would be NBA All-Stars if they played today."

The league finally hit the jackpot two years after the college betting scandals erupted in 1951 when it admitted convicted point shavers who had been banned by the NBA. The likes of Floyd Layne and Ed Roman from City College of New York's infamous 1950 squad that won both the NIT and NCAA, Sherman White of Long Island University, and Ralph Beard and Alex Groza of Kentucky became widely ballyhooed gate attractions. Jack Molinas, a certified All-Star who was booted from the NBA in 1954 for wagering on his team (the Fort Wayne Pistons) to win certain games, was another Eastern League headliner. Several suspected but never convicted dumpers—Bob Zawoluk from St. John's, Bill Spivey from Kentucky—were other attractive curios.

Hubie Brown adds that "The majority of the guys who became great officials in the NBA all learned how to referee in the Eastern League. I'm talking about guys like Earl Strom, Jake O'Donnell, and Mendy Rudolph, whose father by the way was president of the league. One of the early Eastern League refs was Tommy

Lasorda, who later traded in his whistle for a baseball and wound up managing the Los Angeles Dodgers."

Through the years, the Eastern League also featured several over-the-hill players or still-developing youngsters, the most notable being M. L. Carr, Sihugo Green, Art Heyman, Cleo Hill, Bob Love, Mike Riordan, Ray Scott, Paul Silas, Bob Weiss, and Harthorne Wingo.

Meanwhile, the EL had been perpetually hopeful of developing some sort of working relationship with the NBA. But the EL's admittance of so many point shavers in the early 1950s made this impossible. However, by the late 1960s all of the tainted players had retired, and there were some vague preliminary discussions aimed at the NBA's partially subsidizing the EL in return for an as yet unresolved player-development arrangement.

But even this tenuous beginning collapsed in 1974, when the NBA Players Association took notice of the fate of John Brisker, a double-digit scorer for the Seattle SuperSonics, whose lack of off- and on-court discipline irked his coach, Bill Russell. Strictly as a punitive measure, Russell sent Brisker to the Eastern League, where in a handful of games, he averaged more than fifty points. To the Players Association, the EL was henceforth deemed to be a detention hall for unruly players and the interleague negotiations were dead.

Another reason why the NBA shunned the EL was the most risqué trade in the history of professional sports. It seems that the general manager of Team A made an agreement with the general manager of Team B to transfer the rights of a certain player from A to B. However, since Team B had no cash to spare and the EL had no college draft at the time, other arrangements had to be made.

After much dickering the two teams finally agreed to the following terms: the secretary of A's general manager would get together with B's general manager to deliver a blow job at a later date.

One is left to wonder exactly how the transaction was officially recorded.

Then there was the time when a player dissatisfied with his lack of playing time tried to drown his coach in a toilet bowl. Not to forget the similarly discontented player who grabbed his coach's necktie and hoisted him off the ground. Or the coach (Herb Brown) who protested a ref's call (Ken Mauer) by grabbing his whistle lanyard and twisting it until the ref's face turned blue. (It should be noted that neither the other ref, the two coaches, nor the players made a move to come to Mauer's aid.)

Through the years instability remained the most significant constant in the EL: during seventeen of the league's first twenty-one years, at least one team folded or relocated either during or after the season. In 1967 the American Basketball Association came into being and most of the Eastern League's best players eagerly jumped to the new organization, lured by pricey contracts that the EL's teams couldn't come close to matching. At the start of the 1974–75 season, the EL was down to four teams—Hazelton, Allentown, Scranton, and Cherry Hill.

Then in 1976, four American Basketball Association teams joined the NBA, and the remaining five ABA franchises ceased operations. Now there was a return migration of high-quality players back into the Eastern League. A year later, franchises could be purchased for $8,000, and the EL had franchises variously situated in Pennsylvania, Rhode Island, Massachusetts, New Jersey, New York, plus a franchise in Anchorage, Alaska.

The 1977–78 season provided a milestone for the Eastern League. That's when three of its players signed with NBA teams: Harthorne Wingo with New York, Charlie Criss with Philadelphia, and Brad Davis with the Lakers. At the end of that same season, another minor league—the Western Basketball Association—folded, and in anticipation of adding more quality players and far-ranging franchises, the owners of the holdover EL teams convened on August 26, 1978, in Quincy, Massachusetts, to rename their league the Continental Basketball Association and prepare for their suddenly bright future.

Jim Drucker's father, Norm, had been a longtime NBA referee, but Jim was more interested in sports administration. Drucker narrates the strange circumstances that made him the CBA's first-ever commissioner: "The ten owners met with two candidates—me and Steve Kaufman, who's now a high-powered agent operating out of Malibu—in a somewhat sleazy hotel in the worst section of Quincy. The owners didn't want to spring for a rented meeting room, so we gathered in a cocktail lounge where the arguments soon became loud and nasty. Also, there seemed to be an unusual number of flashy but well-used women floating around. During a break in the negotiations, I agreed to meet privately with one of the owners who supported me over Kaufman, but when we entered his room we found a man and a woman fucking in his bed. Anyway, I was confirmed by a vote of six to four. Thirty minutes after we all checked out of the hotel the next morning, the joint was raided by the local police. Turned out the hotel was really a whorehouse."

Prior to the forthcoming 1978–79 season, the hiring of Drucker paid immediate dividends when he negotiated a million-dollar contract with the NBA for "referee development." Most of the money was used to finance the league office in Drucker's hometown of Lafayette Hill, Pennsylvania, with the CBA's franchises each receiving about $75,000. Among the current and/or most recent crop of NBA refs who got their start in the CBA are Derrick Stafford, Bill Spooner, Tony Brothers, Eddie F. Rush, David Jones, Michael Smith, Tom Washington, Gary Zielinski, Mike Callahan, Ken Mauer, Bob Delany, Ron Garetson, Steve Javie, Monty McCutchen, Leon Wood, and Ronnie Nunn.

"The CBA was never about the players, the coaches, nor the fans," said Garetson. "The only reason why the league existed was to provide a proving ground for referees."

No wonder the inmates referred to the CBA as the Crazy Basketball Association.

Through a complicated procedure that centered on his most recent NBA team being the New Jersey Nets, the CBA's rights to Micheal Ray Richardson belonged to the Albany Patroons, the league's showcase franchise. For Steve Warshaw, the general manager for the Rockford Lightning, Richardson's history of drug abuse would definitely not have disqualified him from playing for Albany. "One of the purposes of the CBA," said Warshaw, "is to rehabilitate guys and get them back into the NBA. Since the average annual salary for a CBA player is a little more than $6,000, we like to think players in our league can't afford drugs."

However, if only five or six players got coked out of the CBA every year, the quasi-official drug of the league was marijuana.

Here's what one veteran CBA coach emphasized to his players during their initial team-wide meeting: "The CBA has zero tolerance for coke. One positive test and you're out for good. That means you'll never play in the NBA or over the waters. But the drugs tests here do not test for pot. So, stay away from coke no matter what the circumstances. If you must get high, smoke a joint, but only on off-days or after games. And here's a tip for smoking pot on the road . . . Stuff a wet towel under and above the door to keep the smoke from leaking into the hall. And keep the noise down so the desk clerk won't call the cops. If pot is semi-legal in the CBA, it's still a crime in the real world."

This coach's players greatly appreciated his pragmatism and his honesty. From that point on, there was a bond of trust between him and the most mature of his players.

For the 1987–88 CBA season, the Albany Patroons were coached by Bill Musselman, who had already coached the Tampa Bay–Rapid City Thrillers to three consecutive CBA championships. The fiery Musselman had a history nearly as dramatic and controversial as Richardson's.

Musselman had been a three-sport hero at Wooster High School in Wooster, Ohio. From there he went to Wittenberg College, where he became the second-leading career scorer in the school's basketball history. His coaching career had a modest beginning— leading Kent State University High School to a 14-5 record in 1963. Then came a six-year tenure at Ashland University and an overall record of 109-20.

Even then, Musselman approached the game with a ferociously competitive attitude. He relentlessly drove his players to reach perfection and ruthlessly attacked their every mistake. Winning justified any tactic. Channeling Vince Lombardi, Musselman's mantra was "Defeat is worse than death because you have to live with defeat."

This attitude even applied to his relationship with his son, Eric. "We used to play one-on-one while I was growing up," said Eric, "and Dad always came right at me, playing as hard as if his life was at stake. And he kept on beating me until one day when I was in the ninth grade. After that game, he didn't speak to me for a few days, and we never played one-on-one again."

From Ashland, Musselman moved into the big time in 1971 when he was named the head coach of the University of Minnesota. There, his intensity only increased. He placed a sign bearing his motto over the entrance to the players' showers, and his pregame speeches were designed to drive his players into a frenzy. Despite leading Minnesota to its first Big Ten championship in fifty-three years, earning appearances in the NCAA and NIT postseason playoffs, and finishing his four-year tenure with a 63-32 record, Musselman's career was besmirched by the events of one particular ball game.

In the locker room prior to a February 6, 1972, showdown against Ohio State University in Minnesota, Musselman primed his players by showing them World War II battle scenes—huge guns blasting away from navy destroyers, bombs falling and exploding, machine gun fire, grenades being tossed. As a result, his players were frothing at their mouths, ready to do or die. Despite Minnesota's inspired hustle and desire, the Buckeyes led 50–44 with only thirty-six seconds left in the game. That's when Luke Witte, osu's All-American center, was driving to the hoop headed for an apparently unopposed layup. Suddenly, Witte was body slammed and staggered by Clyde Turner, punched in the side of his head by Corky Taylor, and knocked to the floor. But the vicious assault continued when Ron Behagen began to stomp on Witte's face and neck. Next, Corky Taylor approached the fallen Witte and extended a hand, ostensibly to help the big man to his feet. But just as Witte was nearly erect, Taylor thrust a knee into his groin. Two other Buckeyes were similarly beaten, even as the hometown fans cheered.

Afterward, the Minnesota players blamed Witte: As players from both teams had left the court for the halftime intermission, the Gophers' Bobby Nix thrust a fist into Witte's face. Trying to push the fist away, Witte lightly grazed Nix's face. Corky Taylor claimed that, while he was attempting to help Witte to his feet, the victim spit at him. When slow-motion reruns failed to substantiate Taylor's claim, Taylor backtracked, saying he thought Witte was going to spit at him.

In any case, Witte had to be carried off the court in a stretcher and spent several days in a hospital. An eye injury he suffered negatively impacted his subsequent NBA career.

One osu player, Benny Allison, noted that all of the attackers were black, and all of the victims were white. Allison claimed that he and a black teammate were in the middle of the melee but were ignored by the otherwise bloodthirsty Minnesota players.

Several suspensions were handed down by the Big Ten's administrators, yet Musselman escaped censure. His only response was to shrug and vow that he had nothing to do with the assault.

Indeed, Musselman seemed to be rewarded for the incident when, shortly after the season, he became the coach of the San Diego Sails in the upstart ABA. However, the franchise folded after a 3-8 start, and he moved on to coach the Virginia Squires, only to be fired after compiling a dismal 4-22 record. The next stop was the Western Basketball Association where Musselman led the Reno (Nevada) Bighorns to the finals before losing in the seventh game to the Tucson Gunners. The WBA folded shortly thereafter.

Musselman's next gig was with the NBA's Cleveland Cavaliers. At last, he was being recognized as belonging in the highest echelon of coaches. Unfortunately, he was demoted to director of player personnel after the Cavs went 25-46, and that was his position as the 1981–82 season commenced. But the wheel kept spinning—after Chuck Daly posted a 9-32 record, Musselman made a return visit to the Cavs' command seat. Too bad Cleveland's roster was top-heavy with guys who were much more interested in partying than in hooping. Musselman resigned after winning only two of twenty-three games.

But the carousel continued to spin, and the next fool's gold ring that Musselman snatched enabled him to coach the Sarasota Stingers of the CBA. Fired once again with the Stingers at 6-13, Musselman landed a few miles up the coast with the Tampa Bay Thrillers—and it was there that he finally became a genius, winning three consecutive CBA championships from 1985–87.

For sure, he was a terrific coach, but the real secret to his success in the CBA was Musselman's famous Little Black Book. It contained the contact information of virtually every agent in the business, enabling Musselman to know when blue-chip players would be getting cut from NBA teams or returning from overseas gigs. In the middle of one playoff series against the

Phil Jackson–coached Albany Patroons, Musselman unexpectedly added Coby Dietrich to his roster. Dietrich, a six-foot-ten veteran of thirteen seasons in both the ABA and NBA, proved to be the difference. For the seventh game of another playoff series (also against Jackson's Patroons), Rod Higgins made his first-ever CBA appearance. Higgins, who had already played in seven NBA seasons (and would go on to play in nine more) was at the time a free agent and had just recovered from an injury. With Higgins scoring thirty-seven points, the Thrillers won the deciding game on their way to Musselman's third CBA title.

Several of Musselman's players were never great shakes in the NBA but were game changers in the CBA. Guys like Michael Brooks, Scott Brooks, Tony Campbell, Don Collins, Mario Elie, Steve Hayes, Connor Henry, Kevin Loder, Sidney Lowe, Perry Moss, Ed Nealy, Scot Roth, Linton Townes, Ron Valentine, Clinton Wheeler, Freeman Williams, Kevin Williams, and Ray Williams.

In addition to filling his rosters with superior players, Musselman was also an outstanding coach at this level. Even though zone defenses were still verboten, Musselman's teams played cleverly disguised (and hugely effective) variations of 2-3 zones. His offensive playbook was nearly as hefty as the Manhattan telephone directory. (Flip Saunders, who played for Musselman at Minnesota, was also noteworthy for having a voluminous playbook when he coached in the NBA.) Indeed, Musselman had so many sets and so many plays that opposing CBA coaches had a difficult time preparing a suitable defensive game plan.

Besides his game-time expertise, Musselman sometimes resorted to off-court skullduggery to achieve his goals. The most dramatic of these occurred during a 1985 playoff series against Phil Jackson's Albany Patroons.

Albany's leading scorer and zaniest player was Frankie Sanders. At six feet six and two hundred pounds, Frankie could run, jump, create, shoot the lights both on and off, and play terrific defense when he so desired—which was just about never. And if his head had been screwed on correctly, he could and should have had a long and successful career in the NBA.

He'd been an All-American schoolboy in his hometown of Dayton, Ohio, and was recruited by dozens of powerhouse college programs in 1974. That included Bobby Knight, who was then at Indiana and who, according to Frankie, offered him a hundred dollars per week plus a phantom job. In any event, Sanders wound up at Southern University because "they offered [him] the best deal."

In 1978 Frankie was drafted in the first round (twentieth overall) by San Antonio but lasted only twenty-two games with the Spurs. In almost 12 minutes per game, he shot 39.5 and averaged 6.0 points. "But that's where," Frankie says, "I learned about white drugs and white women."

Musselman's Thrillers had cruised a 144–129 win to open the series in Tampa Bay, but game two was a dogfight. Late in the fourth quarter Frankie intercepted a pass and broke ahead of the field with no defender within twenty feet. However, instead of directly attacking the basket, he swerved to his right so as to pass in front of the Thrillers' bench. Then Sanders slowed down for just a beat as he approached Musselman—long enough to flip Muss the bird and to say, "Fuck you!" Only then did Frankie resume his journey hoopward and defiantly execute an impressive dunk. Sanders ended up with a game-high thirty points in a 113–100 win for the Patroons. There was a minimum of celebrating for the visitors as they hustled back to the hotel to rest up for a 6:00 a.m. flight to Albany the next morning.

But at around 3:00 a.m., the phone rang in Frankie's room. It was Musselman.

According to Frankie, this is what Muss said: "What you did to me was an insult of the worst kind. If you ever do anything like that again, you'll wind up in a hospital."

According to Musselman, this is what he really said: "Congratulations, Frankie. You played a wonderful game."

Before the start of game three in Albany, Musselman made a dramatic entrance into the arena—flanked by a brace of no-necked, muscular, mean-eyed, scowling, three-hundred-pound brutes.

When asked by the Albany media to identify his companions, Musselman just shrugged and muttered something vague about his needing protection after being threatened. He refused to provide any particulars.

During the game, Musselman's two protectors sat just behind the visitors' bench. And Frankie certainly got the message. Not that Sanders said anything. All he did was play timidly and ineffectively, scoring a season's low of six points.

The Thrillers won that game and closed out the series in Albany.

According to another CBA coach, yours truly, more than Musselman's being just a ruthless, scheming monomaniac, he also possessed an admirable sense of fairness—even if it was demonstrated in his own special over-the-top fashion. I was coaching the Savannah Spirits in a game at Tampa Bay. It was a tight game all the way, but late in the fourth quarter, the refs called three dubious charging fouls on my best player, Cedric Henderson, and the Thrillers won on a buzzer-beating shot by the late "Fast" Eddie Jordan. Instead of celebrating his victory, Bill followed the refs off the court to their locker room, screaming that they had "screwed Charley out of the win." He continued to kick and pound his fists on the closed locker room door, raging for another ten minutes. When I caught up with him and tried to calm him down, he said, "If I can't win a game fairly, then I'd rather lose."

Several months later, on November 17, 1987, unannounced and unexpectedly, Micheal Ray Richardson entered the Washington

Avenue Armory just as Bill Musselman was about to conduct his Patroons through the last of their preseason practice sessions.

What did Richardson want?

To try out for the team.

"Okay," said Musselman, "you've got twenty minutes to show me you can play basketball or you're out of here."

At the time, Tim Layden was on hand, covering the Patroons for the *Albany Times-Union*. The highly respected Layden later graduated to a long career with *Sports Illustrated* yet still remembers what transpired during that practice session:

"He was thirty-two and his face was still youthful, but Richardson had been tossed from the NBA nearly two years ago, so he had a noticeable belly. Musselman's guards were Sidney Lowe and Lowes Moore who had been NBA players, plus Scott Brooks who would soon become an NBA player. But, although Richardson could only play about three minutes at a time before taking a blow, he made these guys look like rec-league players. I mean, Richardson just tore them up. I interviewed Richardson right after his tryout, and he was totally humble and sweet. Musselman signed him to a contract the next morning."

Putting his name on a Patroons contract, however, was not easily done. That's because each team in the CBA had a salary cap of $80,000, so the most Albany could pay Richardson was $500 a week. This obstacle was surmounted when Musselman, as was his wont, offered to pay Richardson at least another $500 per week in cash. Because of their considerable investment, the Patroons required Micheal Ray to undergo two random drug tests every week.

Done deal.

Since Musselman had coached the Cleveland Cavaliers and had already won three CBA championships, Richardson believed that playing for him represented his own best chance to get back to the NBA.

So Musselman was the driven, complex perfectionist who would be Micheal Ray Richardson's latest coach. One thing that Musselman was not, though, was Richardson's latest father figure.

Richardson and Musselman got along well to start the season, each one understanding how much they needed the other. They even shared some laughs together. During one all too typical endless wait for a flight, Micheal Ray began to give his imitation of some of the things Musselman says about his players during a ball game.

"Lowes Moore, you're too slow."

"Micheal Ray, you're terrible. Get out of here."

"Scott Brook, will you play some fuckin' defense?"

"Rowland, that's your man."

And, sooner or later, to every player on the team: "I'm going to trade you. You're out of here."

Musselman laughed and said, "Naw, that ain't me."

Richardson also laughed, saying, "Coach, don't fool yourself."

The Patroons zoomed out of the gate winning their first eleven games. Musselman put Richardson in the unusual position of coming off the bench, playing twenty minutes per game at both wing positions. The point guards were Sidney Lowe (who led the team in assists) and Scott Brooks. Tony Campbell was the starting shooting guard, averaging 23.7 points per game until he was called up by the Los Angeles Lakers. At small forward was Derrick Rowland, scoring 19.7 points per game and becoming Micheal Ray's closest friend on the team. Michael Brooks manned the strong forward slot, scoring at a 14.9 clip before being summoned to play with the Denver Nuggets. In the middle was Scot Roth, whose 19.5 points per game average induced the Utah Jazz to add him to their roster.

Coming off the bench, Richardson averaged 13.9 points, 3.1 assists, and 1.6 steals in 26 minutes per game. Only late in the playoffs, after the NBA gleaned the best players from the roster, was Richardson installed in the starting lineup.

One midseason game in Albany caused Musselman to blow a gasket. The night before, the Rockford Lightning (coached by the author) had lost in La Crosse by 139–90. Yet the Lightning then inflicted a 108–107 defeat on the Patroons—Albany's first home loss of the season.

After the game in the locker room, Musselman showered his players with hot-wire screaming curses, accusing them of being losers. He then vowed to make wholesale changes in the roster. (Which he did not do.) To the press, Musselman charged that Rockford's coach had deliberately thrown the game in La Crosse to make Musselman and his players overconfident.

As the season progressed, and the Patroons swept through the league (finishing with a record of 48-6), Richardson began to resent his status as a sub, and his relationship with his coach swiftly deteriorated. A four-time NBA All-Star coming off the bench in the Crazy Basketball Association?

Moreover, Richardson was bored with the inferior level of competition and played hard only in spurts. Even so, Musselman's main beef was that Richardson's play was "too flashy."

While Musselman thought Richardson's on-court antics were showboating, Micheal Ray was simply having fun.

If Musselman routinely verbally abused his players, he did allow Richardson some slack. During one timeout, Richardson made a suggestion about more effectively defending an opponent who was scoring at will, but Musselman's response was, "Shut the fuck up! I'm the fucking genius here."

"Yeah," said Richardson. "Well, f-fuck you."

Musselman ignored Richardson's comeback and plotted his own defensive strategy. The point being that Richardson was the only player Musselman ever coached who was allowed to trade "Fuck you's" with him.

Even so, Micheal Ray was often the object of Musselman's absurd mania for noticing the minutest details: the Patroons had just won a game on the road when the phone rang at 3:00 a.m. in the hotel room that Richardson shared with Rowland.

"It's for you," said Rowland.

It was Musselman, loudly berating Micheal Ray for something he had seen while investigating the game tape.

"When Rowland scored a jumper at the end of the third quarter," Musselman fumed, "everybody on the bench applauded. Everybody except you! I'm watching the tape right now! That's just another example of you being selfish again!"

Flabbergasted, and still half asleep, Richardson said nothing.

Musselman cursed him for a few more minutes, then said this: "Ah! Brooks just scored on a putback and I can see you clapping like everybody else. . . . Okay, you can go back to sleep now."

Oftentimes, though, Richardson had more aggressive reactions to Musselman's routine madness.

In the 1971–72 NBA season, the Los Angeles Lakers set a still-surviving record by winning 33 consecutive games. This was a mark that Musselman desperately sought to surpass even though it might be accomplished in the CBA.

The Patroons were riding a 19-game win streak and had a record of 31-3 when they lost to the home-standing Charleston Gunners. After the game, Musselman once again went off on his players. "You're all fucking losers! Every one of you! Losers! Fucking losers!"

Then he pointed a finger at each of his players, screaming, "What have you ever won? . . . Not a fucking thing!"

One by one, the players hung their heads in sad agreement with Musselman's charges. Then Musselman pointed to Richardson.

"And you! You're the biggest loser of them all! Tell me what the fuck you've ever won? Nothing! Just like the rest of them!"

Richardson lifted his head, looked into his coach's eyes, and said, "You're right. I ain't never won nothing. Nothing except for four fucking NBA All-Star rings."

"Ahh," was all the stymied Musselman could say.

During halftime of another game that Albany was losing, Musselman cursed out his players, then picked up a chair and heaved it across the locker room. Without saying a word, Richardson picked up another chair and threw it to where Musselman's chair had landed.

Speechless, Musselman could only shake his head. *Perhaps*, he might have thought, *Richardson was even crazier than he was.*

On the road, Richardson routinely was the subject of abuse from fans. But in a game in Biloxi against the Mississippi Jets, the wife of Tom Schneeman, the home team's coach, got into the act. As the teams warmed up before the opening tip, she stood up and repeatedly screamed at Micheal Ray, "Just say yes! Just say yes!"

Richardson successfully resisted the urge to tell her to go fuck herself.

Being in the CBA did little to restrain Richardson from indulging his extracurricular appetites: Brian Frucio was Musselman's assistant coach, and as the Patroons took the court after the midgame intermission, Frucio would always raise anywhere from one to four fingers. This was a signal to Tim Wilkin, another writer for the *Times-Union*, as to how many beers Richardson had consumed in the half-time locker room.

Indeed, Richardson was a free spirit who totally resisted Musselman's tightly disciplined game plan.

During the Eastern Conference playoffs against the Savannah Spirits, Musselman threatened to kick Richardson off the team for habitually freelancing and aborting the Patroons structured offense. But the threat was never carried out because Musselman understood that he couldn't win his fourth-straight CBA championship without Richardson.

"Fuck it," said Richardson. "Here I am in the CBA, and I'm going to do what I want to do."

The Patroons cruised into the best-of-seven-games championship round against the Wyoming Wildcatters. The first game was played in Albany and as the Patroons gathered around their coach just prior to the commencement of an overtime period, Richardson was pissed. He had played only fifteen minutes so far despite scoring eleven points on 5-8 shooting. When Micheal Ray was handed a cup of water, he either dropped it or threw it to the floor in disgust. In any event, some water spilled on Musselman's clipboard.

After losing the game, Musselman told reporters that he was inclined to boot Richardson off the team before game two was played.

But Richardson was not cut and scored twenty as the Patroons evened the series. Musselman then told Tim Wilkin that Michael Ray had been benched in game one to motivate him for the rest of the series. "And it sure did work," Musselman smirked.

The series moved to Wyoming, where the Patroons won game three. Up by 2–1, the Patroons looked to gain a stranglehold on the best-of-seven series, and with the Patroons leading by sixteen late in the third quarter, the outcome seemed to be inevitable. Indeed, the early minutes of the fourth quarter were what Tim Layden called "a victory parade." But Musselman couldn't stand his players' showboating.

When Richardson threw a between-the-legs-no-look pass out of bounds, Musselman called a time-out, walked onto the court, and yanked him from the game. With Richardson on the bench, the Wildcatters came back to win the game and even the series.

"After the game," says Layden, "Richardson came over to me and started cursing Musselman. He said Musselman was crazy and had no reason to humiliate him in front of the two thousand fans at the game. That was no way to treat a human being, Richardson said. So that was the story I wrote."

After Layden's story was printed in the next morning's newspaper, Musselman was hopping mad. But instead of complaining to Layden, he called Tim Wilkin.

"He started screaming to me about what a bad guy Layden was," says Wilkin. "I don't know what he wanted me to do about it or what part he thought I had played in the whole thing. But Musselman was off on a screaming, cursing jag. After a while, I put the phone down and went on about my business. About every five minutes, I'd pick up the phone and say, 'Yeah, Bill. I hear you.' Then I'd put the phone back down again. This went on for almost an hour. I mean, the poor guy was unhinged."

With Richardson once again getting minimal playing time, Wyoming won game five. The Patroons returned to Albany having to win the next two games to give Musselman his fourth consecutive CBA championship.

Meanwhile, Richardson kept telling his teammates that, after the season, he would say this to Musselman: "Thank you, Bill, and fuck you!" A promise he never delivered.

With Richardson playing exceedingly well in expanded daylight, Albany did indeed win games six and seven.

However, the very next day, Richardson was the life of the Patroons' celebratory party. And he and Musselman hugged each other like they were big-time buddies.

"Despite all of their disagreements and clashes," says Tim Wilkins, "Musselman and Richardson had the same fiercely driven on-court personalities. Off court, too, both were very personable and easygoing. They were a perfect Jekyll-and-Hyde match."

If Richardson never played another game in the CBA, his connection with the league—and with the Albany Patroons—would eventually resume.

Meanwhile, FIBA had lifted the ban on Richardson, so Micheal Ray's next stop was Knorr Bologna, a division one team in Italy. And his journey over the waters was representative of the solution to David Stern's most pressing problem.

The Great Migration in Black and White

During the 1985–86 season, Richardson's last in the NBA, there were twenty-three teams in the league whose combined rosters included a total of sixty-seven white players. Discounting Mike Smrek and Ron Crevier, who were both born in Canada and played college ball in the United States, as well as Ernie Grunfeld, who was born in Romania, raised in New York City, and was an All-American at the University of Tennessee, only four of these white players were imported from foreign countries: Detlef Schrempf and Ewe Blab from Germany, Petur Gudmondsson from Iceland, and Georgi Glouchov from Bulgaria.

Fast forward to the 2012–13 NBA season, where a total of 101 white players appeared in uniform. True, the league had expanded to thirty teams, yet only 46 of these white players were born and raised in America. The other 55—from Omer Asik to Nicola Vucevic—were essentially foreign imports, and only a handful of them had played collegiately in America. The 2013 NBA draft showed the same tendency: of the 60 players selected, only 8 were American-born whites, while the whites drafted from other countries numbered 13.

In the 2016 NBA draft, five lottery selections were foreign born, as were eighteen of the sixty players chosen. Only five players were American-born Caucasians.

The dramatic increase in foreign whites is no accident. In truth, this was (and still is) a deliberate method of somewhat reducing the overwhelming number of black players on NBA rosters. For sure, a precious few of the current corps of white imports are (or were) outstanding players: Dirk Nowitzki, Kristaps Porzingas, Tony Parker, Manu Ginobili, Luis Scola, Marc and Pau Gasol. Some are average or somewhat better: the likes of Omer Asik, Bogdan Bogdanovic, Marco Belinelli, Marcin Gortat, Timofey Mozgov, and a handful of others. But most are either limited role players or outright stiffs: including Tonike Shengalia, Hasheem Thabeet, Gustavo Ayon, Victor Claver, Jan Vesely, Joel Freeland, Nando De Kolo, and several more.

It's primarily in this last category that foreign whites have displaced black players.

So, then, where do these "extra" blacks go to cash in on their talents?

Mostly countries like Italy, Spain, France, Turkey, Germany, Israel, and lately China. Indeed, according to A. J. Mitnik, a widely respected international scout, as of the 2012–13 season, only four of the top fifty American players overseas are white.

In 1988 Micheal Ray Richardson finally joined the ranks of American blacks playing in what was euphemistically called "over the waters."

Even though Bologna, Richardson's in-season home from 1988–91, is the site of one of the oldest universities in history, the city's nickname is *la grassa*, the Fat. That's because food and other pleasures of the flesh have always been readily available there. Accordingly, the two basketball teams in Bologna have been sponsored by such firms as Eldorado (ice cream), Granarolo and Latte Sole (both producing various dairy products), Kinder (chocolate), PAF (pasta), and Mangiaebeva (literally "Eat and Drink"). No surprise, then, that the sponsor of Richardson's new team was Knorr, an international corporation that produced soups, bouillon, spices, and sauces.

The names of some of Bologna's streets also indicate other more visceral opportunities available there: Vicolo Baciadame (Lady-Kisser Lane) and even Via Fregatette (Tit-Rub Street).

Prior to leaving for Bologna, Richardson had been getting his basketball chops back up to speed by playing in the Houston Pro-Am League along with Moses Malone, John Lucas, and Chris Morris, the Nets top draft choice. He was also enrolled in Lucas's drug rehab program and submitting to three drug tests every week. Prior to signing his contract with Knorr Bologna, and with his two-year's banishment just past, Richardson had also applied for reinstatement into the NBA in February 1988. The league had just completed an intensive investigation during which over two dozen people were interviewed (including his wife Leah), his drugs tests were reviewed (all of them negative), plus he had met with David Stern, the NBA's general counsel, and the league's director of security. All of the evidence led Stern issued this statement: "It appears that Micheal Ray Richardson has constructively dealt with his addiction. No one can be absolutely sure that any recovering addict will not suffer a relapse, yet on the basis of all the circumstances, it is appropriate that Micheal Ray Richardson's application for reinstatement be granted."

The ruling meant that Richardson was eligible to sign with any NBA team that approached him. If he did join another team, his previous NBA team, the New Jersey Nets, would not be entitled for any manner of compensation.

Richardson was thrilled by the news. "I'm grateful for the NBA for giving me another opportunity to play basketball. I'm thirty-three years old and I think I have paid my dues."

Richardson claimed that Philadelphia had made him a sizable one-year offer, but Sugar Ray turned down the 76ers for several reasons: The guaranteed two-year contract he had signed with Knorr Bologna that paid $350,000 annually and the sizeable bonus he was promised if he finished out the season with them. Also the unlikelihood that an NBA team would likewise guarantee him two-year's employment. So, despite his jubilation, Richardson opted to continue his playing career in Italy.

Turned out, though, that the Philadelphia 76ers denied ever having offered Richardson any kind of contract. Did Richardson scam the Bologna team to squeeze more money from them?

In any event, after playing a few games with Bologna, Richardson was impressed: "Italy is a really strong league. I'd say next to the NBA it's probably the second-strongest level of play in the world." Likewise were the fans, the local media, and Bologna's ownership impressed with Richardson.

In his 1994 book on basketball in Italy, Jim Patton observes that Richardson "had more talent than Italians had ever seen." Every time Richardson made one of his routinely spectacular plays, the Bologna fans would chant, "Shoo-gah! Shoo-gah!"

However, the sheer unadulterated fanaticism of the spectators at literally every venue often proved to be dangerous—especially when a visiting team had the audacity to defeat the hometown heroes. As the winner's bus pulled out of the parking lots, dozens of irate fans would routinely gather to throw rocks and bottles at departing foes. After every win on the road, Richardson learned that avoiding a widow seat was a good idea.

Sugar Ray found some other aspects of the Italian basketball culture "crazy." Most imported Americans had to give presents to their Italian teammates or no passes would come their way. There was one Italian coach who made his players run up and down the court while tapping a blown-up balloon as a way of softening their shooting touch.

"Playing in Italy was like stealing money," Richardson said, "but there was no racial prejudice at all. And I gradually began to feel more like a European than an American."

Besides, "There's less crime over here, everybody is way, way more relaxed, and the people are wonderful." So wonderful, in fact, that Richardson divorced Leah and married an Italian woman.

With Richardson's being ably assisted by Clemon Johnson, another black refugee from the NBA, Knorr Bologna won the 1989 Italian championship. Reports of Richardson's stellar play were noted in Philadelphia when the 76ers belatedly offered him a guaranteed one-year contract. "By then I was thirty-four," he says, "and I thought to myself, well, if I went back to the NBA, I might play that one year and that might be it. Since the Sixers wouldn't go for a two-year guaranteed deal, I decided to stay in Italy." Another reason for his decision was Knorr Bologna's extending his contract for a third year.

At age thirty-four, Richardson demonstrated that his basketball chops were still in order during an Italian League all-star game played in Rome on November 26, 1989. With both the north and south squads featuring a total of eighteen former NBA players (including Brian Shaw, Darwin Cook, and Wes Matthews), Richardson dominated the procedures by scoring fifty points, which remains the high-water mark for Italian all-star competitions.

Even though he was playing power forward, Richardson led Knorr Bologna to a second consecutive Italian league championship before spearheading the successful drive to capture the prestigious Cup of Cups awarded to the European champions. But Richardson's competitive fury apparently created at least one major incident.

In the last two minutes of a hotly contested game played on November 25, 1990, between Knorr Bologna and Ranger Varese a wild on-court fight broke out. The riot police were summoned to restore order and twelve players (including Richardson) were ejected. Bologna finished the game with only three players and lost 91–73. In the wake of the brawl, the referees identified Richardson's cursing of the Varese players as the instigating factor. However, none of the banished players were subjected to any fines, suspensions, or any other disciplinary measures.

While it's hard to imagine the NBA not punishing game-time fighting these days, violent mano a mano confrontations have been a large part of the history of the league.

The NBA was called the Basketball Association of America during its inaugural 1946–47 season. (The name was changed to the National Basketball Association in 1949 when the BAA absorbed several teams from the defunct National Basketball League.) The BAA's charter teams were situated in Washington, Philadelphia, New York, Providence, Boston, Toronto, Chicago, St. Louis, Cleveland, Detroit, and Pittsburgh. Five of the franchise owners were associated with National Hockey League teams, and five ran teams in the American Hockey League. Only Mike Uline, the owner of the Washington Capitals, had no connection with a professional hockey team. Moreover, the BAA/NBA's first commissioner, Maurice Podoloff, had previously been charged with administering the American Hockey League.

No surprise, then, that the NBA's founding fathers believed, to a man, that their customers were attracted to ice hockey because, as one sportswriter had it, "I went to a fight and a hockey game broke out." That's why the BAA's referees were instructed to let the cagers batter each other with impunity. If the college game was for boys, the new pro league would showcase a man's game. As a result, in-game fights were routine.

The fact that since no matter how ruthlessly a player was assaulted, the attacker could only be assessed one foul led to many teams recruiting so-called hatchet men. The most notable of these were Vern Mikkelsen (Minneapolis Lakers, 1949–59), Wally Osterkorn (Syracuse Nationals, 1951–55), and Bob Brannum (Boston Celtics, 1951–55). In later years, these practitioners of the hard, knock-'em-down foul were called "enforcers" and included the likes of Bill Laimbeer, Rick Mahorn, Xavier McDaniel, Charles Oakley, Gene "Bumper" Tormohlen, "Jungle" Jim Luscotoff, John Q. Trapp, Maurice Lucas, and many more.

Accordingly, the history of the NBA includes numerous dramatic fights. Here's a list of the most notable combatants:

Bill Russell versus George Dempsey on February 19, 1959.

Wilt Chamberlain versus Sam Jones on April 1, 1962, wherein Jones grabbed a photographer's stool to keep Chamberlain at bay. In that very same game Carl Braun and Guy Rodgers also exchanged punches.

On February 21, 1963, Clyde Lovellete punched out several of Wilt Chamberlain's front teeth, causing the big fellow to ponder retiring from the NBA.

The dishonor roll also includes a pair of coaches (Red Auerbach and Harry Gallatin) exchanging blows and having to be separated by the Boston police. Other brawlers included Hall of Famers Richie Guerin, Walt Bellamy, Oscar Robertson, Willis Reed, Kareem Abdul-Jabbar, Tom Heinsohn, Rick Barry, Neil Johnston, Phil Jackson, Connie Hawkins, and Cliff Hagan. Plus various bloodbaths variously involving the Philadelphia 76ers, Portland Trail Blazers, New York Knicks, Los Angeles Lakers, Houston Rockets, Milwaukee Bucks, Atlanta Hawks, Boston Celtics, Phoenix Suns, Sacramento Kings, Indiana Pacers, Chicago Bulls, plus the "Bad Boy" Detroit Pistons fighting just about everybody.

It should be noted, however, that there was a racial aspect to virtually every NBA punch fest. In July of 2011, an enterprising website—pbrbasketball.blogspot.com—listed all of the on-court fisticuffs that occurred from December 27, 1960, to November 21, 1969. Of the fifty-four on the list, only five pitted black players against each other:

Al Attles versus Zelmo Beatty (April 12, 1964) matched two of the most belligerent players in the history of the NBA.

The otherwise peaceful Leroy Ellis traded blows with McCoy McLemore (November 7, 1964) and also with Joe Caldwell (November 28, 1965).

Beatty and Bill Bridges teamed up to assault Jim "Bad News" Barnes on March 8, 1967.

And Lew Alcindor was involved in a two-for-one battle against Bob Rule and John Tresvant on November 21, 1969.

All of remaining fifty-one brawls involved either white-on-white or black-on-white combatants. It's only very recently that the black brothers in the exclusive NBA fraternity have felt liberated enough to occasionally pound on each other.

Yet a pair of game-time fights have garnered the most attention, the most horrific of these being Kermit Washington's smashing Rudy Tomjanovich's face (December 9, 1977). The other critical incident took place in Detroit on November 24, 2004, when a fight between the Pistons and the Pacers spilled into the stands.

For sure, blame the BAA's original owners for trying to attract erstwhile hockey fans by institutionalizing game-time violence. But there are several other reasons why subsequent NBA action has historically included so much bloody hand-to-hand combat:

More than any other professional sport, too many NBA players then and now are victims of their own self-perceptions. For them, the importance of being mucho-macho takes precedence over other, more significant values—like fair play, compromise, honesty, open-heartedness, respect for the game, and appropriate behavior. Too bad this "man's man" image is a phony one.

For the true warrior, self-restraint is the ultimate measure of courage and self-respect. Not unleashing an elbow to the face in revenge for a careless insult. Not returning a hip check with a take down.

That's because true self-respect comes from the inside and is projected outward. If the proffered insult is patently false—if the intended victim is not a "pussy," a "weakling," a "coward," a "motherfucker," or whatever he might be called—then the true warrior disregards it. His ultimate identity cannot be influenced or altered by what opponents think of him or do to him.

Those putative NBA he-men who overreact to the most marginal of slights are merely demonstrating how shallow and tentative their image of themselves as true warriors really is. Case in point—during a game played in Houston on February 2, 1995, Vern Maxwell ran into the stands and punched a fan who he later claimed had been heckling him. The Rockets' guard never disclosed the nature of, or the reason for the fan's verbal abuse—and Maxwell was assessed a ten-game suspension and a $10,000 fine.

Even more infamous were the hostilities between the Pistons and the Pacers in Detroit—known as the Malice at the Palace—on November 19, 2004. This brouhaha was initiated when Indiana's Ron Artest (later to be called Metta World Peace) committed a hard foul from behind on Detroit's Ben Wallace. The Pistons' big men responded by shoving Artest, and the altercation accelerated when a fan threw a partially filled cup of beer at Artest. That led to Artest and his Pacers teammates Jermaine O'Neal and Stephen Jackson leaping into the stands and attacking several fans.

If Wallace were a true warrior, he would have laughed at Artest's childish behavior and concentrated on making his free throws. But Wallace believed he was dissed, insulted, chumped and became a victim of his own false self-image.

Likewise did Artest believe himself to be so demeaned by the trash that the fan threw at him that his only reaction had to be immediate retaliation. By so doing, Artest proved himself to be too weak to avoid assaulting a hapless civilian. Count Jackson and O'Neal in the same misguided category.

In truth, suffering the slings, arrows, and beer cups launched by outrageous fanatics is part of an NBA player's job description—but overreacting is not. Do the math. A cup of spilled beer plus some punches landed on civilians wound up costing nine players a total of 146 game suspensions as well as $11,548,832 in salaries lost.

And what's the reason why so many NBA players are so quick to take offense when they believe their manhood is being challenged? Because the media, the NBA publicity machine, and the league's various corporate sponsors present the players as supermen. Bigger than life—ours, and even theirs. Buy the sneakers they wear or a facsimile of their game jerseys, eat their favorite snacks, drive their favorite cars, and even the clumsiest, nerdiest among us can bask in the shadow of real manhood.

It's all a scam, and the players are bigger suckers than anybody else.

But why, then, are the most passionate fans such willing victims? Because their workaday lives are usually so empty, frustrating, and unfulfilled that they desperately need some kind of vicarious experience to make them feel like winners. Too bad the anger and resentment of their personal realities is always there just beneath the surface of their painful grins and strained good cheer. It's a coiled sort of anger that is constantly being repressed. Would they dare vent their profound discontent to their spouses? Or their bosses? Hell, no.

So one of the reasons why Sports America is populated by so many millions of devout fans is that rooting for a particular athlete or team is an acceptable way of releasing that anger.

However, rooting for the good guys often means rooting against (and demonizing) the bad guys.

Notice, though, that all of the fans involved in the Malice in the Palace brawl were sitting in some of the most expensive seats in the arena. Perhaps, in our current spiritless culture, having the material pleasures that money can buy is not enough to bring peace unto one's soul.

In truth, the Detroit Debacle was the NBA's worst nightmare come to pass. The "flagrant foul" rule was instituted around the time of Maxwell's grievous transgression, but it was not ultimately designed to prevent the players from assaulting each other. Along with the thinking of the original BAA bigwigs, player-on-player mayhem is still considered to be boffo at the box office. Yet, by instituting severe penalties for on-court contact that might precipitate fisticuffs (and by punishing bench-bound players who mount the court to enter the fray), the NBA was hoping to prevent such fights from spilling over into the stands. Imagine the litigation should any of the wealthy courtside fans be accidentally injured!

Uh oh!

The bottom line is that the corporate entity that is the NBA is a victim of its own need to generate big ratings and big bucks. By lionizing individual players and thereby marginalizing the importance of teamwork, the league necessarily creates artificial heroes and villains, true believers and apostates. Both the idolatry and the ill will that result have distorted the purity, grace, and even the beauty of The Game.

What to do, then? How to bring a sense of proportion into the business and fanaticism of professional sports?

Education is the only answer—or rather, reeducation. The players, the fans, the professional observers, and even the NBA's puppet masters must learn how to discern the true, transcendent beauty of athletic competition. In truth, basketball is ballet with defense. A leaping, dancing, spontaneous celebration of the human spirit as performed by gifted, acrobatic giants—the finest athletes in the world! The Game represents a blending of skills in unlimited and unpredictable combinations. Yes, it's five against five. But it's also ten players playing one game.

Winning is certainly the goal. But so is community of spirit. And there's also a bittersweet glory in playing the right way and losing. Both on and off the court.

But, alas, the bean counters who really run the NBA will only evaluate their sport in numbers inked in red or black.

In any event, Richardson's foul-mouthed instigation of the free-for-all in Varese was never mentioned by Knorr Bologna's administrators as the reason for his fall from grace after the 1991 season, his third in Italy. Instead, the team's management made the ridiculous claim that Richardson was cut loose only to clear salary space to sign a better player.

Richardson, however, had his own interpretation of why the team declined to renew his contract: "The coach was an ego maniac, and he resented the fact that I was a bigger star than he was."

Lorenzo Sani was a sportswriter for the local daily *Il Resto del Carlino*, the most prestigious newspaper in Bologna. (Consistent with Bologna's eat-drink-and-be-merry culture, the name of the newspaper translates as "change from the cost of an espresso.") Sani had this to say about the move: "Sugar had a great year and is still the most popular player in town. Because it seems like such a crazy decision, there is the impression that it has to do with drugs. And because of Sugar's past, nobody asks for any further explanation." While, it was generally believed that Richardson had failed some drug tests, Sani had his doubts. "I say if there is evidence, let's see it, if there is none, this is really crazy. But there is nothing Sugar can do. He is gone from Bologna. And he's most angry at Alessandro Mancaruso, the general manager of the team." Sani parenthetically noted that Mancaruso was infamous for having "a very big nose."

In response to Sani's skepticism, Mancaruso claimed that Richardson did, indeed, fail a drug test administered by the team. Mancaruso added that Richardson's "basketball career is probably over." (Richardson did indeed test positive in his latest drug test.)

Gary Bettman, the NBA's senior vice president and chief counsel, said that the news meant that Sugar Ray's reinstatement into the league was retracted: "If, in fact, Micheal Ray Richardson has suffered a drug relapse, he would not be eligible to participate in the NBA."

Joe Taub was dismayed by this latest development. "It was a real sad day for me when I heard," said Taub. "I regret that I've lost contact with Micheal Ray, but I want to talk to him. I want to help him."

Taub's reaction speaks volumes about how Richardson's buoyant, endearing personality so strongly affected people who knew him well. If it was easy to get angry with Richardson, it was impossible to dislike him. Yet if some opportunities were no longer available, Richardson was still an extraordinary basketball player. In short order, he signed a one-year deal with KK Split, a traditional powerhouse team in Croatia.

The most notable alumni of Richardson's latest team were Dino Raja and Toni Kukoc, who were both born in Split and went on to successful careers in the NBA. Drazen Petrovic, born in nearby Sibinek, was another outstanding performer for KK Split before excelling in the NBA. The team had won several Euroleague competitions, and in the McDonald's Championship tournaments in 1989 and 1990, Split had survived into the title games—first losing to the Denver Nuggets by 139–129 in Rome, then being bested by the New York Knicks. 117–101. Even so, the overall level of play was not quite up to the standards of the Italian teams.

Split was the second largest city in Croatia (ranking only behind Belgrade, the capital city), and its placement along the eastern shores of the Adriatic Sea made it the country's most popular tourist attraction. Beaches, thermal spas, world-class golf courses and restaurants, ski slopes, the ancient ruins of the medieval quarter, plus lively nightclubs all ensured that Sugar Ray, for one, would enjoy his stay there.

Yet all the benefits of playing and living in Split were overshadowed by the spreading war in the Balkans. As the fighting drew closer to Split, Richardson grew more apprehensive and began to think about making a quick exit stage left. However, since the hostilities were mostly kept at a distance during the season, he did finish it out.

In any event, Richardson hadn't been in Croatia for a month when, by sheer happenstance, a European Cup game matched Split against his former team from Bologna. Because of the war, the game was played in La Coruna, Spain. Revenge was on his mind, so before the game Richardson browsed through the local marketplace and came up with the perfect object to accomplish his desire: a pair of thick black eyeglasses topped with bushy black eyebrows and attached above a huge plastic nose. A nose nearly as big as the one on Alessandro Mancaruso's face.

After the game, which Richardson iced by converting a pair of late-game free throws, he donned his eyeglasses-nose apparatus and marched around the court waving a "STOP THE WAR IN CROATIA" sign that accompanied the team wherever they played. Then Richardson found Mancaruso and sprayed his ex-boss with a storm of curses in English and Italian. Forever after, Richardson referred to that specific contest as "the big nose game." (Interesting to note that Richardson never stuttered when speaking Italian.)

Yet despite Richardson's gaining a huge surge of satisfaction, Split failed to win any international competition, and besides, the encroaching war made a prolonged sojourn in Split unrealistic. Because his most recent positive drug test had been administered by Knorr Bologna and not by the Italian League, Richardson was eligible to play for any other Italian team that desired his services. So it was that the next stop on Richardson's basketball caravan was a return trip to Italy—this time with Baker Livorno.

Another port city boasting gorgeous Mediterranean beaches, tony hotels, restaurants, and night clubs, Livorno was a short drive from Florence. If Richardson's newest team was notably better than his last team, Livorno was far from being among the Italian League's elite ballclubs. Except for Richardson, the other once-and-future NBA players who played for Livorno included Lee Johnson, Scott May, David Wood, Anthony Jones, Jay Vincent, and Brad Wright—all of them strictly marginal performers.

The highlight of Richardson's two-year stint in Livorno occurred late in the 1992–93 season when he was instrumental in defeating heavily favored Knorr Bologna by 83–81 in overtime at Bologna. With the still loyal Bologna fans chanting, "Shoo-gah! Shoo-gah!" Richardson tallied thirty points, mostly on isolation plays out of a 1-2-2 set.

However, with the team mired in the lower depths of the standings, and with its financial difficulties leading to a bankruptcy procedure, Richardson decided to move on.

Next up was the Olympique Sharks situated in Antibes along the French Riviera in southeast France. Richardson was the first ex-NBAer to wear a Sharks uniform and was succeeded by only two more—Brad Sellers in 2000, and David Rivers in 2005. However, the forty-three golden beaches, super-luxurious accommodations, the Picasso museum, the Napoleon museum, and world-famous jazz festivals have lured several megacelebrities to live in Antibes for extended periods—the likes of Graham Greene, the Duke of Windsor, and Aristotle Onassis. If Richardson was not quite an international icon, he did lead the Sharks to the French championship in 1995.

At the time, the most competitive basketball was played in Italy, Spain, Turkey, Greece, and the Balkan countries with France relegated near the bottom of the list along with Germany, Belgium, and Holland. Yet in times to come, a slew of NBA players would claim France as their birthplace or be proud to be French citizens. This list includes Tony Parker, Nicolas Batum, Bruce Bowen, Udonis Haslem, Ron Anderson Jr., Boris Diaw, Ronny Turiaf, Rodrigue Beaubois, Joakim Noah, Evan Fournier, Mickael Pietrus, and J. R. Reid. Would it be too much of a stretch to believe that Richardson's dynamic performances provided a significant impetus for the growth of basketball in France?

In any event, while Richardson at age forty was still an incredibly dynamic player able to command midlevel six-figure salaries, in 1996 his status as the best American hooper in Europe was eclipsed by Dominque Wilkins's signing with a team in Greece. Wilkins was only thirty-five and justified his $3.5 million contract by leading Panathiakios to the Greek Cup and the Euroleague championship. Then Wilkins returned to the NBA with the San Antonio Spurs for the 1996–97 season. A year later, Wilkins played for Bologna before finishing his NBA career with Orlando in 1998–99.

Meanwhile, Richardson was continuing his own basketball odyssey. After three seasons in Antibes, he played the 1997–98 campaign with another French team (Cholet Basket).

In October 1997 Richardson was in attendance for the McDonald's Open, a preseason tournament in Paris that featured the Chicago Bulls. NBA commissioner David Stern was also on hand, and Richardson was eager to make a connection. "I sat next to him," Richardson recalls, "and I told him that he saved my life by opening my eyes and getting me back on the right track. His eyes just lit up. Here was the guy who had ended my NBA career, but I did not hold any grudges. Ever since then, we've had a special relationship." In truth, Stern did more than save Micheal Ray Richardson's life—he rescued the NBA from becoming strictly a second-rate attraction.

According to Bill Walton, a counterculture quasi-hippie, "David Stern is the single most important person in the history of basketball."

Stern was born on September 22, 1942, in the Chelsea section of Manhattan "when a sense of neighborhood and family community was important," he says. "My father owned and ran a grocery store, and it was always a big deal when he got free tickets to a baseball game from one of his beer suppliers. I was a die-hard Giants fan, so Willie Mays was much better than Mickey and the Duke. I also liked the Giants because they had the first all-black outfield with Willie Mays, Hank Thompson, and Monte Irvin."

The young Stern was also a Knicks fan, and he favored playing basketball over any other sport. "I played on my synagogue team," he says. "Then when I went to college at Rutgers, I played in the Teaneck rec league. But I never had any delusions of being a real player. I was a reliable defender, and if I ever did wind up with the ball, I'd pass it quickly to someone who could shoot. Playing basketball was always fun."

After graduating from Rutgers, Stern enrolled in the Columbia Law School, passed the New York State bar in 1966, and was immediately hired by Proskauer Rose, an influential law firm. For the next twelve years, Stern functioned as the NBA's "outside counsel," before becoming the league's general counsel in 1978. When Larry Bird and Magic Johnson were drafted in the spring of 1979, Stern was instrumental in changing the entire focus of the NBA's publicity machine. Instead of concentrating on The Game, Stern encouraged the promoting of individuals, i.e., Magic and Bird. "Either you move ahead and stay with the times," Stern explained, "or you fall off the chart."

Within two years, Stern was the NBA's executive vice president and was the driving force in establishing mandatory and random drug testing, as well as a salary cap. Both of these innovations were so appreciated by the team owners that on February 1, 1984, he was made the NBA's commissioner.

During his thirty-year tenure as the administrative face of the NBA, Stern succeeded in implementing several other actions that further enhanced the league's popularity: When Michael Jordan joined the Chicago Bulls in 1984, a carefully crafted publicity campaign resulted in His Airness succeeding Magic and Bird as the NBA's most iconic player-personality. Stern convinced the NBA's board of governors that the coin flip used to determine which of the league's two worst teams would get the number-one draft pick was a cheap trick. Thus began the search for a suitable draft procedure that would discourage teams from tanking games to obtain better picks.

Under Stern's impetus, the NBA expanded from twenty-seven to thirty teams, and added a third referee to each game.

Violet Palmer and Dee Kantner became the first female referees in any major U.S. sport.

The several McDonald's classics, routine exhibition games played by NBA teams against European opponents, and the admittance of NBA Dream Team into the 1992 Olympics, all led to the increasing influx of white Europeans into the league.

Stern was the guiding force behind the establishment of the Women's National Basketball Association.

Before Stern's regime, the NBA finals were televised on tape delay. Within five years, the finals were shown live on network TV.

Under Stern's guidance, the NBA became the first major sport to utilize cable TV.

Not counting ticket sales, the twenty-seven teams that existed in 1985 garnered a combined total of about $20 million in outside revenue. By 2014 that income had ballooned to $5.5 billion.

The NBA instituted a systematic use of instant replays to correctly adjudicate several carefully categorized close plays.

Stern implemented a dress code for players, forcing them to wear business suits or conservative attire to and from arenas while representing their respective teams.

Stern flexed his influence in December 2011, when—acting as de facto owner of the league-controlled New Orleans Hornets—he vetoed a trade that would have sent Chris Paul to the Lakers, Pau Gasol to the Rockets, and Lamar Odom to the Hornets.

It was Stern's banishment of Micheal Ray Richardson—"the hardest thing I've ever done"—that virtually ended the drug abuse scandals that had plagued the NBA.

And the "life-saving" bond between Stern and Richardson proved to be a lasting one. Before every season that Sugar Ray played in Europe, he and Stern made sure to connect via lengthy phone calls.

However, Stern's tenure as commissioner did contain some serious missteps—including five "lockouts" by the owners in their continuing attempts to weaken the NBA players' union. In 1995, 1996, and 1999, these procedures didn't last long enough to affect the forthcoming seasons. But the 1998–99 campaign was reduced to fifty games and the 2010–11 season to sixty-five games.

Both of these abbreviated seasons led to skewed results because the surviving games had to be squeezed into a briefer schedule. With teams required to play four games every week instead of the usual three, ballclubs centered around older players were severely handicapped. Plus, the historical and statistical continuity of the NBA was utterly disjointed.

Another of Stern's low points was his permitting the annual highlight video of the 1988–89 season to focus on the "Bad Boy"

Detroit Pistons. "What happened," he later said, "is that one of the NBA's merchandising partners came to me after Detroit's first championship and proposed that the NBA's home video be called 'Bad Boys.' The guy said he was losing his behind in video sales, and he felt that the outlaw appeal would boost marketing. Besides, everybody was calling the Pistons 'Bad Boys' anyway. So I went along with it."

Of course, the glorification of violence eventually led to the dreadful fight at the Palace five years later. Clearly, antiviolence measures had to be instituted.

Under Stern's impetus, subsequent rules mandated the automatic expulsion and suspension for any player who threw a punch, whether the blow landed or not. Also, any player who left the bench and stepped onto the court during a melee would likewise be suspended. But more subtle changes were deemed necessary.

Hand checking was outlawed, said Stern, "because it slowed the game and encouraged a bump-and-grind style. Plus, everybody was getting annoyed. Slap that hand away, push it away, push it back. And that's not what fans were paying to see."

Besides lowering the players' temperature and hopefully preventing physical confrontations, the ban against hand checking diminished the effectiveness of individual defense. So, too, did prohibiting a defender from bumping off-ball cutters.

Another reason for penalizing physical defense was to really give the fans what they "were paying to see." More flashy uncontested dunks, and much more scoring.

With offensive players now granted the freedom to move in the attack zone, NBA coaches had no trouble adjusting to the new game plan since Euroball offered a ready-made model: Continuous cutting through the paint, snappy ball reversals around the perimeter, employing guards and wings who were comfortable driving and kicking, an emphasis on three-point shooting, and a general concern with spacing the floor. Also, since the vast majority of fouls are called on the defense, high pick and rolls as well as pick and fades not only generated open treys but allowed the refs a clear view of isolated action that only involved four players.

As a corollary, the refs began to permit ball penetrators to take an extra step, hop, skip, and/or jump as they approached the basket. Virtually incapable of being defended in one-on-one situations, this maneuver was even called the "Euro Step."

Meanwhile, after playing for one rather lackluster season for Cholet Basket, Richardson returned to Italy with Carne Montana Forli (1998–99), a team named for its sponsor, a meat company. "The competition is better in Italy," Richardson explained, "and so was the money." At forty-three, Richardson was twenty-two years older than his youngest teammate.

Richardson then decided on another one-season go-round in Livorno, followed by reprising his stint in Antibes (2001), and finishing his active career with another French team AC Golfe-Juan-Vallauris in 2002.

Here's what Richardson had to say during his last season as a hooper: "I was put out of the NBA because of drugs, but you know what? I always wake up and kiss my blessings. Here I am sixteen years later, and I'm still playing professional ball. Still doin' my thing. So I ain't mad at nobody. All I ask is that you be real. Don't paint me out to be no choir boy, because I wasn't. Just judge me for what I was able to do on that basketball court, nothing else. That's all I ask. Because where there's muthafuckin' shit, there's always some muthafuckin' sugar."

However, if Richardson had long harbored the goal of being the oldest professional basketball player in the world, his retirement at age forty-seven left him five years short of the European career of Ron Anderson Sr.

If Richardson's playing career was over, David Stern found a way to get Micheal Ray back into the NBA.

Back in the USA

Stern made a call to Kiki Vandeweghe, the Denver Nuggets' general manager, encouraging him to hire Richardson as part of the Nuggets' community-relations team. Five months before this, Richardson had encountered Vandeweghe at the Euroleague finals in Bologna, where he spoke about his yearning to return to the States. Having been impressed with Richardson, Vandeweghe responded quickly to Stern's prompting, and Micheal Ray returned to the NBA and to his hometown. Richardson's family now included his third wife ("my last one," he vowed) and their two children.

Richardson called himself a "communications ambassador" whose duties included fundraising for local charities and delivering antidrug lectures and fundamental-skills instructions to youngsters at basketball camps, to junior-high-school and high-school teams, YMCA groups, resident homes for troubled youths, and wherever else his message would be both welcomed and useful.

"The strongest message is talking to them about what I went through. Life and drugs don't mix. I let the kids know that I was a great basketball player, and I got in trouble being in the wrong places at the wrong times, hanging out with the wrong people. I tell them that they've got to pick and choose the people they hang out with and the places they go."

Basketball fans between the ages of thirty-five and fifty remembered Richardson's All-Star play, and according to Deb Dowling, the Nuggets' vice president on community relations, he was "revered" by them. If most of the troubled youngsters were unaware of Richardson's NBA career, he always managed to "inspire" them. All told, Dowling said that Sugar Ray was "unbelievable."

After an appearance at the Excelsior Youth Center, a live-in home for at-risk girls, Richardson's talk elicited this response from Kathy Gravely, one of the resident counselors: "His journey is and will be very inspirational to our girls because our girls are at the Center because they have hit bottom. He explained that he had also hit rock bottom, and that until you do it yourself, you can't improve or get better. You can't keep blaming other people."

For a while, Richardson liked his new job: "It's going real, real well. It's a lot bigger and more satisfying than I thought it would be. I'm getting a lot of positive feedback. I think I'm already affecting lives. The kids I've spoken to are very excited. I'm already beginning to reach out and touch a lot of people."

However, the past intruded on Sugar Ray's idyllic existence in the person of Billy Jack Richardson, his father. When Billy Jack left his wife, Micheal Ray, and his other children, he eventually moved in with his mother "someplace" in Texas. But Billy Jack's mother had recently died, so one of Micheal Ray's brothers felt compelled to fetch his father and bring him to Denver.

"I see him now, once or twice a week," Richardson said. "To tell you the truth, it feels kind of strange. My father, he wasn't there, but he's still my dad. . . . It is what it is."

Perhaps the unexpected presence of his father made Richardson uncomfortable in Denver. Perhaps he got bored with making virtually the same speech so often to so many different groups. In any event, after being a civilian for one season, the lure of The Game qua game became increasing alluring.

This is a normal syndrome for ex-NBAers who because of age or injuries are no longer able to play professional-caliber basketball. They miss the drama, the camaraderie, the spotlights, the high-wire competition, the money, the groupies, the sense of being a full-fledged member of one of the world's most exclusive fraternities. They miss exploring and decoding the secret alphabet of Xs and Os.

Life on the sidelines is repetitive, flat, meaningless, and relatively anonymous. Without it being broken down into recognizable segments of three, eight, and twenty-four seconds, along with twelve and forty-eight minutes, time seems to be too open, too casual, too obscure. Without having to deal with incompetent and/or biased referees, there are no bad guys to rail against.

That's why Richardson longed for Vandeweghe to move him to the Nuggets' bench as an assistant coach. "That would be fantastic," Micheal Ray said. "I think I have a lot to offer, especially to young guards. Not only on the floor, but also off the floor." Unfortunately, the staff of Denver's coach Jeff Bzdelik already was stocked with experienced assistants—most notably Doug Moe, Scott Brooks, Michael Cooper, and Adrian Dantley, all NBA veterans. But Richardson was intent on having his latest dream come true.

In early February 2005, Richardson was with the Nuggets when the team arrived in New York for a game against the Knicks. He was sitting in a courtside seat watching the end of a Knicks practice when he was urgently summoned by Isiah Thomas, New York's president. The Knicks were huddled around Thomas and Herb Williams, the interim coach who had recently replaced Lenny Wilkens.

The Knicks were suffering through a disastrous season. They had just returned from a West Coast trip that featured their inability to maintain late-game leads, thereby losing several games they should have won. After losing eighteen of their last twenty-one games, their current record was a dismal 19-31.

A bad season in New York is always a minicatastrophe for the entire NBA. Because the preseason TV schedules routinely and irrevocably planned for several broadcasts of games played by the team situated in the media capital of the world, sad-sack Knick teams translated into poor ratings. Which is why, perhaps, it was widely believed that the 1985 draft had been rigged (by way of a crease in the envelope that David Stern "blindly" picked) to ensure that Patrick Ewing wound up in New York.

Richardson was also concerned with the Knicks fortunes. "I'm a Knick at heart," he confessed. As such, he had watched the team play whenever they appeared on national TV and carefully studied all of the box scores. His opinion was a variation of his most famous quote: "Right now, they just have their heads above water, and they're definitely sinking."

With Williams's acquiescence, Thomas asked Richardson to speak to the team. Richardson, who was not so secretly itching to become an assistant coach in New York, was totally agreeable.

"What you guys have to do," Richardson said, "is to think positively. Winning as well as losing are both contagious. When you lose so many times, you get frustrated and make little mental mistakes, mistakes that snowball and cost you games. You guys are good enough players to win, but your trouble is only mental. Just be positive and play with confidence and your season will turn around."

Speaking for his teammates, Penny Hardaway voiced his appreciation of Richardson's message: "Coming from a guy like that, you have to respect that, and you have to take that to heart.

Nothing he said was really news to us, but it was helpful to hear it from him."

Richardson's encouraging words perhaps made a difference since the Knicks stepped up and played .500 ball (18-18) for the rest of the season.

And the act of just being in a team huddle and getting such a positive reaction from so many battle-hardened professional players, made Richardson finally understand that public relations was not his gig.

He'd been clean for fourteen years. If he couldn't be an assistant coach in the NBA, then his next choice was to be a head coach someplace else. Because of his past indiscretions, it was clear that colleges would shun him. Anyway, why would he want to dumb down what he knew about basketball and spend the rest of his career coddling hooplings who could barely tell the difference between an X and an O? Not to mention the smiling and all-around sucking up that was such a vital part of recruiting.

Richardson remembered what Bobby Knight had famously said about trying to convince high-school kids to come play for him at Indiana: "The worst thing about recruiting is having a seventeen-year-old kid absolutely ruin your day."

The View from the Bench

The only coaching option available was the CBA in general and the Albany Patroons in particular. Team president Jim Coyne understood that bringing back the colorful Richardson would create a tidal wave of publicity and hopefully attract enough paying customers to put the Patroons back in black ink. Moreover, Coyne personally identified with reclamation projects, simply because he was one himself. In 1992 Coyne was the Albany County executive when he was convicted of bribery, conspiracy, extortion, and mail fraud for accepting a $30,000 bribe from an architect whom he eventually selected to design an all-purpose arena in downtown Albany. Coyne, who insisted that he was innocent, served a four-year stint in a federal prison.

"I saw a lot of ruined lives in prison," Coyne said. "I saw a lot of people who had lost hope in their futures. Having been there myself, I understand what it can be like to be passed by and then offered a second chance in life. I had read a newspaper article about Micheal Ray and his interest in coaching, and I thought this is a guy who, if given a chance, might just succeed. I thought I could help him."

Given this golden opportunity, it remained to be seen whether or not Richardson could coach CBA players, a group that one disgruntled CBA coach called "hardened criminals."

In addition to sending a host of players to the NBA, the CBA had also been a training ground for NBA coaches. Of course, the list of NBA head coaches who had served their apprenticeship in the CBA is headed by Phil Jackson, who coached the Patroons from 1983–87. Others are Flip Sanders, Eric Musselman, Keith Smart, Dennis Johnson, and Brendan Suhr. CBA head coaches becoming NBA assistants include Mark Hughes, Gerald Oliver, Mo McHone, Cazzie Russell, Paul Mokeski, Darrell Walker, Bob Thornton, Henry Bibby, and Kevin Mackey.

Eric Musselman: "The experience gained by coaching in the CBA for one season is equivalent to five years' coaching in the NBA. That's because a CBA coach always has to be extremely flexible. We had to coach to the available personnel and be prepared to adjust our game plan to suit the most unexpected circumstances. Players suddenly getting called up to the NBA or leaving without a warning for gigs overseas. So the most important skill that I brought with me into the NBA was concentration. No matter what happened, no matter how crazy things got, I was able to concentrate on the next play, the next substitution, the next game. Once I got into the NBA, things like injuries, personnel changes, and wacky players acting out didn't faze me that much. After coaching in the CBA, the NBA is a piece of cake."

Phil Jackson: "Coaching in the CBA made me a much more flexible coach in the sense that I had been too rigid in my player rotations and too obligated to players who had performed well for me in the past. A crucial part of my development was learning how to go with the flow of a ball game."

Flip Saunders: "I liked the camaraderie of being around the players so much and getting to know them. Because we all had the same goal of getting into the NBA, we realized that we needed each other to get there, and that brought us all very close together. It gave me a model of behavior that I tried to implement when I coached in the NBA. Also, the CBA was where a coach could experiment and try out different concepts without the multimillion-dollar NBA pressure of having to win every night."

Jim Sleeper was a twenty-year man, having coached the Grand Rapids Hoops, the Maine Lumberjacks, the Bay State Bombardiers, and the Sioux Falls Skyforce. "For all its quirks, the CBA game was more real, more human, and much more fun than the NBA's dumbed down, arrogant, me-first version. Notice, too, that the only teams who played an interesting, intricate style of basketball were all coached by CBA refugees."

Pete Myers has been an assistant coach for several NBA teams. "I played in the NBA for eight years, and I found that most of my coaches there (except for Phil Jackson) were very aloof from the players. Like we were the reluctant schoolboys and they were the righteous principals. But when I played in the CBA, I discovered that most of those guys were so hands-on and fun that we were eager to follow their instructions. That's when I decided that my future was to become a coach. And the kind of coach that I wanted to be was modeled after the guys I played for in the CBA."

On the negative side of the ledger, Tom Nissalke, Dave Cowens, Bob Hill, Herb Brown, and Joe Mullaney were NBA head coaches who finished their coaching careers in the CBA, while Bill Musselman and George Karl bounced from the NBA to the CBA and then back to the NBA.

Whatever the opportunities for advancement might have been, coaching in the CBA was often unusually challenging and sometimes even hazardous.

Bill Klucas: "I was the coach of the Anchorage Northern Knights, and in the middle of the 1979–80 season, we embarked on what I'm sure was a record-setting road trip that lasted thirty-

THE VIEW FROM THE BENCH

two days. We flew into Rochester, New York, and from there on we traveled everywhere else in a van that I had to drive. Every article of clothing we brought had to be either hand-washed in a motel sink or not washed act all. It's not surprising that some of us got on each other's nerves. I'd estimate we had about a dozen blood-letting fistfights."

A few years later, Klucas was coaching the Rochester, Minnesota, Flyers, and at the tail end of the 1987–88 season, his team was being routed by Rockford. There was a brouhaha during halftime that could be overheard in the adjacent visitor's locker room. It seems that there was a soda dispenser in the home team's locker room, and during Klucas's halftime excoriation of his players' effort, David Thirdkill (an NBA vet) walked over to the apparatus and started filling a paper cup with soda. Seeing this, Klucas freaked out. Because of their miserable performance so far, there'd be no soda for the players.

"Don't tell me what to do, motherfucker!" said Thirdkill.

"I'm the goddamn boss here!" insisted Klucas.

"You ain't shit!" Thirdkill said as he continued filling the cup. Whereupon Klucas reached over, reached out, and knocked the half-filled cup to the floor.

Thirdkill reacted by grabbing Klucas in a headlock and threatening to punch his face to jelly.

The other players took a few moments to consider the situation. Eventually, a few of them interceded and broke up the melee before Thirdkill before could actually start punching away.

Klucas was fired later that night. And guess who was named the interim coach?

David Thirdkill.

If Thirdkill never again played in the CBA, Klucas survived to coach several more CBA teams over the years.

Sometimes the abuse CBA coaches suffered was verbal: Frankie Sanders had been San Antonio's top draft pick out of Southern

University in 1978, but his NBA career lasted for only sixty-eight games in abbreviated stints with the Spurs, the Celtics, and the Kings. Still, he was Albany's leading scorer in 1983–84 when Phil Jackson led the Patroons to the CBA championship. Sanders believed that his ticket back into the NBA depended upon how many points per game he averaged. To make this happen, Sanders felt he should be playing forty-eight minutes in each and every game. That's why, whenever Jackson removed him from the action, Sanders would shout, "You son of a bitch! You're messing with my game!" If most of the fans on hand heard Sanders's loud complaint, Jackson thought it best to never respond.

Back in the late 1980s Dave Cowens was coaching the Bay State Bombardiers and became increasingly annoyed when his opposite number, Bill Musselman, jumped up and down as he loudly complained to the refs when even the most noncontroversial calls went against him. Finally, without saying a world, the six-foot-nine Cowens approached the five-foot-eight Musselman, grabbed him by the lapels of his trademark blue leather sports jacket, lifted him off the floor, and shook him until Musselman was as limp as a rag doll. Still wordless, Cowens then dropped Musselman to the floor, then calmly returned to his seat on the Bombardiers' bench. The referees were laughing too hard to hit Cowens with a technical foul—and Musselman subsequently confined his elocutions to whispered instructions in his team's huddles.

After the game, Cowens had nothing to say to the media, but Musselman did—claiming that Cowens was one of his best friends.

In April of 1986, Jackson's Patroons were on the verge of being swept in a playoff series. The fourth game was being played in Albany, and the competition was fierce. The result was a 113–112 series-ending win by the visitors with the balance being tipped by a horrendous last-second call by one of the refs. As soon as the final buzzer sounded, Jackson's accumulated frustrations overflowed as he grabbed a folding chair and hurled it onto the court. It was his last official act as a CBA coach.

Herb Brown: "Nobody wanted to be in the CBA. Not the coaches, not the players, not the referees. That's why we were all pissed off all of the time."

And even in its halcyon days, the CBA itself was always on the verge of disaster.

Jay Polan, longtime owner of the Rockford Lightning: "The operating budget of most CBA teams was $1 million per season and buying a new or old franchise cost about $800,000 in the golden age of the early and mid-1980s. From the NBA contract we each got about $20,000, enough to cover our league dues. There was no TV money, and we had to pay for the radio broadcasts of our games by selling advertisements. Some of our income came from signs and banners posted around the arena that we sold to local businesses, also ads in our yearbook, team T-shirts, logos, trinkets, and the beer concessions. But our primary source of revenue was gate receipts. At Rockford, our break-even attendance was about four thousand, and our average attendance was about thirty-five hundred. The franchises in La Crosse, Wisconsin, and Gary, Indiana, usually made money. The rest of us lost anywhere from 250K to 400K every year. Owning a CBA franchise was either a tax write-off or an expensive hobby. But, for a while there were always wealthy businessmen ready to buy and bring a CBA franchise into their cities because they were positive that the other owners were knuckleheads and that only they knew how to turn a profit."

Joe O'Hara owned the Patroons for five years: "Here's how to make a small fortune . . . Start with a big fortune and buy a CBA franchise."

However, the CBA that Richardson rejoined was much different than the CBA he had left seventeen years ago. One major

factor was a radical decline in fan attendance due to the prolif-
eration of NBA games on cable TV. The other negative influence
was Isaiah Thomas.

It's indisputable that Thomas was a truly great player—one of the
best point guards ever to play in the NBA. He was the quarterback
of the Detroit Pistons back-to-back championships in 1989 and
1990. However, he was despised by most of his opponents for
being one of the baddest of the Bad Boys. Indeed, one of Thomas's most despicable maneuvers was to deliberately step on the
plant foot of an opponent just as he was intending to become
airborne to shoot a layup, thereby creating the distinct possibility of inflicting a career-ending injury. Thomas's habitual cheap
shots were the primary reason why Michael Jordan refused to
be a member of the original Dream Team that cruised to a gold
medal in the 1992 Barcelona Olympics if Thomas was also selected.

In any event, Thomas's post-playing career was an unmitigated disaster.

Immediately upon his retirement, "Zeke" was the executive
vice president of the newly created Toronto Raptors. During the
four years there, the Raptors averaged a mere twenty-two wins per
season. The season after Thomas quit, Toronto made the playoffs.

Next up for Thomas was being the head coach of the Indiana Pacers, a team that had just lost to the Los Angeles Lakers
in the NBA finals. With virtually an intact holdover roster, the
Pacers won fifteen fewer games in Thomas's first year at the
helm. Indiana continued to underachieve for the duration of
Zeke's three-year stint in the command seat, and when he was
replaced by Rick Carlisle in 2003, Indiana advanced to the Eastern Conference finals.

In 2006 Thomas became the coach of the New York Knicks.
After a miserable 33-49 season, the team's befuddled owner, James
Dolan, rewarded his incompetence by promoting Thomas to the

dual title of president–general manager. Once ensconced in the ultimate power seat, Thomas made a series of disastrous player moves. But the capper of his time in New York was being found guilty of sexually harassing a former employee of the organization, a verdict that ultimately cost the Knicks $11.6 million.

Thomas's involvement with, and destruction of, the CBA dated back to 1999 when he purchased the league, including the arena leases, the basketballs, the uniforms, and jock straps for the sum of $10 million. His motivation was totally rational: the NBA was looking to establish a minor league that would serve as a farm system for the big-league teams, a training situation for prospective NBA coaches and referees, and a place where young players could develop their games.

Since the CBA already had in place everything that the NBA seemed to require and would enable a smooth, speedy implementation of David Stern's plan, Thomas's $10 million gamble had every chance to be a profitable one.

Two weeks after he became the impresario of the CBA, Thomas unilaterally cut players' salaries by one-third, his rationale being that making the "CBA a younger league" would increase its appeal to the NBA. Thomas also made the rounds of the CBA franchises, promising financial support and also using his smiling media persona to create a steady diet of publicity in each city.

In March 2000, the NBA offered Thomas $11 million for the CBA, but wanting much more of a return, Zeke refused. Three months later, Thomas was offered the head coaching position in Indiana, the caveat being a rule prohibiting an NBA coach gaining an unfair advantage in player procurement by owning a league. Thomas responded by signing a letter of intent to sell the CBA to the NBA Players Association, a transaction that never took place.

One month later, the NBA announced that it would establish its own minor league, the National Basketball Development League. With that announcement, the CBA instantly became worthless. In

October, Thomas signed the CBA into a "blind trust" that sealed the books of every team in the league and prevented them from paying their bills. Three months after Thomas became the Pacers head coach, the CBA folded and declared bankruptcy.

Even before Thomas's purchase of the CBA, the once-profitable Albany Patroons were hemorrhaging money. That's why in 1992 team owner Joe O'Hara accepted the sponsorship of a local car dealership and changed the team's name to the Capital City Pontiacs. Too bad what was left of the Patroons' fan base was totally alienated. O'Hara was forced to sell the Pontiacs to a group of Connecticut businessmen who relocated the franchise to the Nutmeg State. When the Hartford Hellcats failed to catch fire, the team folded after two seasons and the rights to the franchise were dormant.

Several businessmen decided to resurrect the CBA in 2005, with the league's flagship franchise being reconstituted in Albany. Coaching the Patroons seemed to provide the only opportunity for Richardson to get involved with professional basketball in his home country.

Despite Jim Coyne's enthusiasm, Richardson's best friend was puzzled. Otis Birdsong and Sugar Ray had been buddies during Richardson's four-year tenure with the Nets. "Of all the guys I played with throughout my career," said Birdsong, "Micheal would be the last one I would have chosen to say he wanted to get into coaching." Indeed, the accepted knowledge was that in his playing days Richardson was the Anti-Coach.

So, then, upon his return to New York's capital city, what kind of CBA coach would Micheal Ray Richardson turn out to be?

Of the many coaches he had played for, Richardson mostly modeled his approach after Bill Musselman. This meant establishing a close enough relationship with agents to compile a Black Book that tracked the comings and goings of NBA veterans and other blue-chip players. Who among them were headed overseas? Who were returning to the States? When? And why? (Poor play, difficulty adjusting to the strange culture, positive drug tests, financial shakiness of the team, and so on.)

Being a Musselman disciple also mean being harsh and demanding with his players. Berating them in team huddles for misplays caused by "brain lock," screaming at referees, and above all being a stickler for the rules.

So, during a road game against the Pittsburgh Xplosion in Richardson's first season on the Patroons command seat, one of the home team's players was whistled for his seventh personal foul. According to CBA rules, Richardson's Patroons were entitled to shoot a technical foul and then retain possession. However, when the refs neglected to award Albany the opportunity to shoot the mandated free throw, and even though the game was already safely won, Richardson violated the boundaries of the coach's box as he stalked them and showered them with fiery abuse. As a result, Richardson was hit with a T, and Pittsburgh was awarded a freebie instead of the Patroons.

Throughout his rookie season as a head coach, Richardson also followed Musselman's footsteps in strenuously objecting to the numerous petty aspects of what amounted to business as usual in the CBA:

Richardson was steamed when he discovered that the Maryland Green Hawks played their home games in a high-school gym that featured a cozy schoolboy three-point line.

Sugar Ray went berserk upon realizing that one corner of the court in Buffalo was dark because of a burned out overhead light.

Nor did he quietly accept the fact that, whereas each home team was supposed to supply five towels for the visitor's bench, in Quebec there were only two.

He also publically voiced his distress when, for several home games back in Albany, some glitch in the laundering process forced the Patroons to wear their home yellow jerseys with their away green shorts.

Unfortunately, Richardson also reprised Musselman's habit of refusing to shake hands with opposing coaches after games that the Patroons lost. Indeed, Sugar Ray's game-time behavior was so tempestuous that several league officials chastised him and warned that the continuance of his antics would force them to fine and suspend him.

Why, then, had Musselman gotten away with such abusive behavior? Because, no matter how over the top he'd been, he possessed an honorable discharge from the NBA, whereas Richardson was an outlaw.

Richardson deviated from Musselman's habitual game plan only in his simplified offense. Instead of the dozens of sets and hundreds of plays that Musselman used, Richardson's Patroons employed a simple series of high pick and rolls, plus some down picks, and low-post play. Because of the high turnover in personnel in Richardson's return to the CBA, his playbook could easily be mastered by newly arrived players in a single practice session.

Even though they failed to make the playoffs, Richardson was hailed as a near genius for coaxing his team to a semirespectable record of 20-28.

Before returning to Albany for the 2006–7 season, Richardson revealed that he yearned to live and work in Europe—particularly in France, where his wife and two children remained during the CBA seasons. He vowed that his second CBA season would be his last. His dream job was to operate as some NBA team's European scout. "Until then," he said, "I'll do my job. When it's over, it's over, and I'll move on. I'm a survivor."

But what indeed turned out to be Sugar Ray's last go-round in the CBA was fraught with even more trouble than he could have imagined.

Derek Rowland had been Richardson's teammate with the 1988 CBA champion Patroons. The amiable Rowland had begun his professional basketball career in 1982 when, in addition to working fulltime flipping stomach burgers at a local McDonald's, he was hired by Phil Jackson to be the Patroons' practice player at twenty-five dollars per week. From there, the sweet-shooting, defensive-minded Roland blossomed into a perennial CBA all-star. Subsequently, a chronically sore knee greatly impaired his effectiveness during a brief stint with the Milwaukee Bucks in 1986. Rowland's active career ended in 2000, but since his Jones still itched, he was happy to accept Sugar Ray's offer to be the Patroons one and only assistant coach.

With Rowland on the bench for every game, the Patroons won twelve of their initial fifteen, then the CBA suddenly changed the rules. The new dispensation gave each team a choice: either bring ten players and no assistant coach on the road, or bring nine layers and an assistant. Richardson was outraged . . . again. It seemed obvious to him and to Rowland as well that the overnight ruling was aimed to hamper the Patroons. Perhaps the CBA littlewigs couldn't abide the possibility of Richardson leading his team to a championship. Just think of the negative publicity! But because of the fulltime up-tempo pace Richardson had instituted, he absolutely needed to have ten players at his disposal.

Rowland reports that, despite the normal CBA craziness, Richardson was much calmer than he had been the season before. However, there were still signs that Sugar Ray might still have been up to his old destructive tricks.

"In February," Rowland says, "Sugar simply disappeared for a few days, leaving me to coach the team for a couple of games. When he came back, he offered no excuses, and I guess we were all too afraid to ask him where he'd been and what he'd been doing."

THE VIEW FROM THE BENCH

In addition, Richardson missed two games to work a fantasy camp in Las Vegas (with Darryl Dawkins) during the NBA's All-Star weekend. Nobody in Albany's front office was pleased.

Meanwhile, Richardson had consulted general manager Jim Coyne about the possibility of making a trade for Marvin Phillips, a power forward with Pittsburgh. According to the CBA bylaws, Coyne was the only person in the Patroons' organization who was authorized to sign, waive, or trade a player—and Coyne was dubious about adding Phillips. "Micheal pretty much assured me that the trade was not going to happen," said Coyne, "so I went to the Bahamas for a week. When I returned to Albany, I learned that Richardson had invoked my name and gone through with the trade."

In response to Coyne's public complaint about being undercut by his coach, Richardson had this to say to the *Albany Times-Union*: "This isn't the YMCA. Are you kidding me?"

It was too late for Coyne to rescind the deal—especially since Phillips's first appearance with the Patroons, he scored a ton of points in a runaway win over the Indiana Alley Cats. After the game, Richardson said to Wilkin, "Do they still want to criticize my moves?"

Bizarre and downright illegal trades were common occurrences throughout the checkered history of the CBA.

The most one-sided exchange occurred in 1988 when the coach of the Rockford Lightning (Charley Rosen) traded a stone-handed seven footer to the Tri-Cities Thunder for an official sweat suit. Tuned out that the player in question hit a critical basket that beat Rockford in an important game just a week before he was cut. And the Thunder sweat suit was much too small to fit the six-eight Rosen.

Still another highly unusual trade was precipitated by the flight of a paper airplane: In the middle of the 1987–88 season, the Wyoming Wildcatters were in deep financial trouble. Their host city—Casper, the Friendly Ghost Town—simply lacked the population to support a CBA team. Desperate to boost their gate, the Wildcatters' owners decided to run a sensational halftime giveaway.

During the midgame intermission, a brand-new Chevrolet sedan was driven out to center court. The center page of every two-dollar program was stamped with numbers unique to that specific program. The fans were invited to pull out the center page, fashion it into a paper airplane, stand anywhere they wished along the sidelines, and launch their missile toward the car. The first one that flew through the open sunroof would win the car.

The car dealer had assured the Wildcatters' management that such accuracy was virtually impossible, especially if the arena's ventilation grids were tilted just so and the fans turned on full blast.

Of course, one lucky spectator defied the odds.

The team owners were aghast, and so was the car dealer.

What could be done?

To refuse the car to the winner would immediately cause the franchise to fold. The dealer, in his desire to keep the Wildcatters in town, agreed to sell the car to the team for $5,000.

The very next day, the Wildcatters contacted the league's wealthiest team and allowed the Rockford Lightning to buy their best player—center Brad Wright—for the five grand.

Wright only lasted in Rockford for six games before being called up to the Denver Nuggets where he remained for the rest of the season. And the Wildcatters continued to operate on a shoestring, losing huge amounts of money before ceasing operations after the subsequent season.

So, even though Micheal Ray's transgression was a comparatively minor one, a serious rift had developed between Jim Coyne and the coach he'd gone out on a limb to hire.

Another area of friction between Coyne and Richardson was even more personal. "Coyne's wife was babying all the players," said Richardson. "At one point, I just told her I didn't want her in my gym, in my locker room, messing with my players."

Richardson then brushed off all of Coyne's objections. "Part of my recovery," said Micheal Ray, "is to tell the truth. I have to be honest with myself and honest with other people. Sometimes it gets me in trouble, but that's just the way it is. It's either yes or no. There ain't no in-between."

If Coyne was looking for a reason to get rid of Richardson, his controversial coach soon presented him with a dramatic excuse.

Sunk Once More

In late March 2007, the Patroons were losing at home in the opening game of the CBA's championship series when a courtside fan began heckling Richardson. Burning with frustration, Richardson shouted, "Shut the fuck up!" As the game neared its conclusion, another heckler was on his case. This time, Richardson's response was even more offensive: "Shut the fuck up, you faggot!"

Surprisingly Jim Coyne said that he had no intention of reprimanding Richardson. "He's an adult and he should know better," said Coyne. "He knows if he's acting appropriately or in appropriately."

But Coyne was no so sanguine the next morning when the *Times-Union* printed a pregame interview with Richardson. The topic under discussion was the possibility that Coyne would offer Richardson a contract to coach the summertime version of the Patroons in the United States Basketball League. Referring to the chance that contractual negotiations might be tricky, Richardson said this: "I've got big-time lawyers. I've got big-time Jew lawyers."

His interviewer then suggested that Richardson's casual remark might be offensive because it supports the stereotype that Jews are shrewd and crafty.

Richardson scoffed at the suggestion. "Are you kidding me? They've got the best security system in the world. Have you ever been to an airport in Tel Aviv? They're real crafty. Listen, they are hated all over the world, so they've got to be crafty."

And why were they hated?

"If you really think about it, everybody knows that the Jews are running the country. Which is not a bad thing, you know what I mean?"

How are they running the country?

"They got a lot of power in this world, you know what I mean? Which I think is great. I don't think there's nothing wrong with it. If you look at most professional sports, they're run by Jewish people. If you look at a lot of successful corporations and stuff, more businesses, they're run by Jewish people. It's not a knock, but they are some crafty people."

The response was immediate—from Coyne to the Anti-Defamation League, Richardson was denounced as a bigoted, homophobic, anti-Semite. Richardson quickly issued an apology, whose sincerity was tainted by his insistence that the second heckler was drunk. A few days later (March 28), Jim Coyne suspended Richardson for the remainder of the championship series, as well as prohibited him from watching the team both practice and play.

Richardson was aghast. He pointed out that his ex-wife was Jewish, that his two children from that marriage were being raised Jewish, and that his Jewish lawyer laughed at any suggestion that Sugar Ray was anti-Semitic. Richardson said that since all of his children had white mothers, he could more justly be charged with being antiblack.

A host of noteworthy writers were quick to come to Richardson's defense.

Christopher Isenberg, a Jewish writer who had profiled Sugar Ray for the *Village Voice*, posted a blog titled "Jews for Micheal

Ray," saying, "Micheal Ray is proud to have a Jewish lawyer because he thinks they are the best lawyers. Certainly it's a stereotype, but it's a stereotype rooted in reality. A disproportionate number of the great lawyers in America are Jews. A disproportionate number of the great basketball players in America are black. We have to be very careful around these facts because here the line between fact and 'stereotype' can get very blurry, and if you're not careful, you can get into deep water real quick. Micheal Ray was unwise to have been so indiscreet around reporters, but it wasn't exactly Elders of Zion territory."

Also coming to Richardson's defense was Zev Chafets, the highly respected and influential author of *A Match Made in Heaven: American Jews, Christian Zionists and One Man's Exploration of the Weird and Wonderful Judeo-Evangelical Alliance.* After dismissing any ill intent in Richardson's characterization of Jews as "crafty," Chafets wrote the following in the *Los Angeles Times*: "What other hurtful things did Richardson supposedly say? That Israel has the best airport security in the world? This is both true and something Israel itself brags about. That Jews are hated and need to protect themselves? That's the founding premise of the Anti-Defamation League. . . . Richardson, who was a popular player in Israel during his NBA exile years, is guilty of nothing more than free speech. Even if his observations were wrong—which they are not—there's nothing insulting about them. What is insulting is the notion that you can't speak honestly about Jews without getting into trouble."

David Stern was likewise moved to defend Richardson, conceding that Sugar Ray's remarks about homosexuals were "inappropriate and insensitive" and worthy of a suspension. Yet, said Stern, "I have no doubt that Micheal Ray is not anti-Semitic. I know that he's not. . . . He may have exercised very poor judgment, but that does not reflect Micheal Ray Richardson's feelings about Jews."

Even the Jewish father of Richardson's most recent ex-wife rallied to his defense. Yet his most vigorous defense came from the *Nation of Islam Sportsblog*, which claimed that it was acceptable to attack certain facets of black culture, that is, rap music, the "misunderstandings" that black NFL players have suffered at the hands of the law, and the antics of what's called the "Black KKK." But being in any way critical of Jews will brand a non-Jew as being a rabid anti-Semite. And, after all, "What IS untrue about what he said???"

The *Sportsblog* then proposed a solution to Richardson's situation: "So, Micheal Ray, head to the temple and shake hands with a rabbi. That will show that you love Jews and want to be rehabilitated. But don't mention that you might be the victim of racism."

Yet the most definitive and sensible analysis of this latest imbroglio was provided by *New York Post* basketball columnist Peter Vecsey, who felt that Richardson was "so unsettled, so unsophisticated and so pliable anybody could draw him into saying anything about anything at any time."

A few short years later, the NBA fined several players for making gay slurs—Kobe Bryant ($100,000 in 2011), Amar'e Stoudemire and Joakim Noah ($50,000 each in 2012), and Roy Hibbert ($75,000 in 2013). But even though all of these NBA gents had much higher public profiles than Richardson did in the CBA, no suspensions were issued.

In 2007 Tim Hardaway, a one-time NBA All-Star, spewed forth some toxic antigay comments to a sportswriter. Since he was no longer associated with the NBA, the only penalty that the league could dispense was to bar Hardaway from participating in the forthcoming All-Star weekend extravaganza. However, at the time, Hardaway was employed by a CBA franchise—the Indiana Alley Cats—as their chief basketball advisor. Within a few days of Hardaway's slurs, Indiana fired him.

Why did the CBA react so strongly to Richardson and Hardaway when the NBA punished the same transgressions only with fines that look to be so incredibly large but only amount to a mere pittance of the guilty NBAers multimillion-dollar paydays?

Because the CBA was decidedly a relatively obscure minor league forever pursuing the illusion of legitimacy.

Moreover, given that Major League Baseball, the National Football League, the Canadian Football League, the Major League of Soccer, and even a prominent rugby club in Australia had either lightly fined or totally ignored similar remarks by their athletes indicates that gay bashing was not a capital crime.

At the same time, though, Richardson's opinions of Jews in general and Israel in particular (whether or not they were willfully anti-Semitic) were most likely the primary reasons for Jim Coyne's strong reaction. That's because Jews are (and always have been) major factors in both the on- and off-court doings of the basketball universe.

Even though the origin of basketball was 100 percent Christian—invented by Dr. James Naismith at a YMCA training school in Springfield, Massachusetts, just before Christmas 1891—the sons of second-generation Jewish immigrants adopted the game as a means of quickly assimilating into the American culture. This was particularly the case in New York City, where half of the country's Jewish population lived. If the vast spatial demands of baseball and football made these activities unsuitable for the city's crowded slums, basketball was seen as an acceptable alternative to such disreputable urban entertainments as were available in dance halls, nickelodeons, and amusement parks. At the dawn of the twentieth century, socialist, labor union, YMHA, and Zionist organizations sponsored hundreds of Jewish teams in dozens of Jewish leagues, all aimed at keeping immigrant youths off the streets and out of trouble. The scarcity of large basketball courts in New York put a premium on passing and cutting, leading this idiosyncratic style of play to be called "Jew Ball." Within a decade of Naismith's invention, the slums of New York (and to some degree Philadelphia) became celebrated as "the centers of the basketball universe."

The league that later became the NBA (in 1949 when it merged with the National Basketball League) began operations as the Basketball Association of America in the fall of 1946. The BAA's first president was Maurice Podoloff, whose immigrant parents spoke only Yiddish. Except for Eddie "The Mogul" Gottlieb, Podoloff and all of the other franchise owners had hockey backgrounds and were unfamiliar with basketball. But Gottlieb's decade's long experience with the famous SPHAs made him the sole source of the theories and practices of basketball in the BAA's board of governors.

Since there was no college draft prior to that initial 1946–47 season, the eleven charter teams were free to sign any players who had graduated, been expelled from, or never attended college. Three distinct patterns emerged: Signing veteran players who had played in any of the extant pro leagues—the National Basketball League, the American Basketball League, the Eastern Professional Basketball League, plus a host of others that were soon to be defunct. Signing as many nationally known college All-Americans as possible. Or focus on signing guys who were born, raised, or played in the vicinity of any given franchise.

The New York Knickerbockers settled on the last option, stocking their roster with players familiar to the prospective local fans—mostly players from CCNY, LIU, and NYU. No surprise, then, that Sonny Hertzberg, Stan Stutz, Oscar "Ossie" Schectman, Leo Gottlieb, Ralph Kaplowitz, Nat Miltzok, Jake Weber, and Hank Rosenstein were all Jews. So it was that a New York Jew from CCNY made history.

The first game in NBA history was played on November 1, 1946, with the home-standing Toronto Huskies downing the New York Knickerbockers, 68–66. And the first basket was scored by New York's sturdy point guard, "Ossie" Schectman.

Despite Schectman's milestone bucket, the Knicks playing to full houses and having a (barely) winning record, the preponderance of Jews on the team (including four of the five starters) eventually created a problem.

That's because the owner of both the Knicks and Madison Square Garden was Ned Irish. Even worse, the coach was Neil Cohalan, a hoops hero at Manhattan College (which was actually situated in the Bronx) and a notorious alcoholic. Cohalan's job was to keep the power seat warm for one season until Joe Lapchick's contract with St. John's would lapse. Yet as the season unfolded, Cohalan became convinced not only that were his Jewish players too cliquish but that the virulent anti-Semitism the Knicks faced on the road intimidated them to the point where their performances suffered.

On a January trip to Pittsburgh, the fans greeted the visitor's appearance on the court by singing their own version of a popular song: "East Side, West Side, here come the Jews from New York." In other cities, when the Knicks had the ball, the fans took to shouting, "Abe! Pass the ball to Abe!"

After Schectman suffered a season-ending injury, Cohalan and Irish quickly traded away five of the remaining Jews. The most impactful of these deals involved Ralph Kaplowitz, who proved to be the necessary catalyst that propelled Gottlieb's Philadelphia Warriors to the league's first-ever championship.

There was a more blatant example of anti-Semitism in that inaugural season.

From the get-go the Pittsburgh Ironmen was a dysfunctional team. Coach Paul Birch's game plan included screaming at his players, kicking water coolers, and being ferociously unhappy with every missed shot, botched pass, defensive lapse, and not only every loss but often with what he believed to be sloppy victories. Yet for some reason that Moe Becker couldn't quite figure out, Birch always seemed to single out Becker for the most virulent abuse. No matter how many points Becker scored, assist passes he made, rebounds he grabbed, or defensive stops he accomplished, Birch always found grounds for criticism. Becker became increasingly resentful, but because he was only a marginal player, he felt that keeping his mouth closed was necessary to keeping his job.

The touchy situation finally came to a violent boil on November 30, 1946, when the Ironmen were playing the home-standing Washington Capitals. The game was extremely physical with a total of forty personal fouls being called.

Here's Becker's version of what happened: "Irv Torgoff was with the Caps, and he was having a field day. Nobody could guard him, including me. Birch was always riding opposing players, and several times he yelled at called Torgoff, calling him a 'kike.' I resented this and I cursed at Birch from my seat on the bench."

Birch kept after Torgoff, who responded with a few choice words of his own. Their argument escalated until they swapped a few punches in the waning moments of the game. The refs quickly banished both of them.

"Birch was already there when the players came into the dressing room after the game," Becker said. "I was so mad that I was ready to attack him, but two of my teammates grabbed me, lifted me up, and put me in the shower to cool off. When I came out, Stan Noszka started to tell me that Birch didn't mean what he'd said to Torgoff as an anti-Semitic remark. By then, I was totally crazy. I thought that Noszka was siding with Birch, so I squared off against him. The other guys pleaded with Birch to break us up, and not let us start throwing punches. Birch just sat back and said, 'Let the Jew take care of himself.'"

Red Auerbach was the coach of the Capitals, and he later but-tonholed Becker in the hallway. "I was so mad," said Becker, "that I was crying. Red told me that if Birch released me, he'd find a spot on his roster for me." Which is precisely what happened. No surprise that Becker was a better player for a Jewish coach than he was for Birch.

In the succeeding generations, the NBA showcased several outstanding Jews: Hall of Famers Dolph Schayes, Red Auerbach (who among his other noteworthy achievements, singlehandedly integrated blacks into the NBA), Larry Brown (the only coach in history to win championships in both the NCAA and the NBA), and Red Holzman (a veteran of the settlement houses who revived Jew Ball and coached the Knicks to a pair of NBA championships).

Also several Jews of ill repute: A Jewish referee, Nate Mes-senger, was universally believed to have been consorting with gamblers to insure Philadelphia's title in 1946. During the 1954 season, another Jewish referee—Leo Hirsh—was banned from the NBA when definitive proof was discovered that he was fixing games in league with gamblers.

In 1954 Jack Molinas was booted from the NBA for gambling on games. In partnership with the Mafia, Molinas went on to be a key figure in arranging fixed games for the next several seasons. He was eventually assassinated by the Mafia.

Despite this often unsavory history, anti-Semitism was virtually unknown during Micheal Ray Richardson's NBA career. That's because David Stern and Adam Silver (his deputy commissioner and eventual successor) were Jewish. As were some franchise owners, for example, the controversial Mark Cuban (Dallas Mav-ericks), the stentorian Jerry Reinsdorf (Chicago Bulls), the volatile Mickey Arison (Miami Heat), the unassuming Lawrence Tanen-baum (Toronto Raptors), the stubborn Herbert Kohl (Milwaukee Bucks), as well as Melvin and Herbert Simon (Indiana Pacers).

Why so many Jewish owners?

According to Nathaniel Friedman, the reason is that "Jews love basketball. If you asked a Jewish millionaire what they really want, he'd probably say they want to buy the New York Knicks. I'll bet they even dream about doing this. . . . Owning a team is a confluence of two Jewish traditions—love of basketball and being good at business."

Additionally, during Richardson's nine-year NBA career, he only played against three Jews—Joel Kramer, Dan Schayes, and Ernie Grunfeld.

Why the drastic reduction of Jewish pros since the BAA's inaugural season?

The admission of blacks into the league (in 1954) and the fact that upwardly mobile young Jewish athletes no longer had a desperate need to assimilate or escape a ghetto by playing basketball. Playing tennis and/or golf was more fitting for these youngsters.

Ah, but anti-Semitism, like racism, is permanently embedded in many aspects of American culture. And if Bill Russell experienced blatant acts of racism while playing for the Celtics, Boston was also a bastion of anti-Semitism. For sure, the Celtic faithful adored Red Auerbach but only because of his record-breaking successes as the team's coach and president. Irv Levin, however, who was a co-owner of the Celtics from 1975 to 1978, was never a fan favorite. According to Levin's son, Lon, there were many fans who did not like the idea of a Jew owning their team. They showed their displeasure by booing Levin every time he showed his face in the Boston Garden.

Rather than being an unpleasant vestige of the past, there are still traces of anti-Semitism alive and unwell in the NBA.

For example, just before the NBA's 2012 draft, here's what an anonymous scout's private opinion concerning the prospects of a professional career for the University of Pennsylvania's Zack

Rosen: "I just don't see it. I can't get past the red hair and the Jewishness."

Still, Jim Coyne had another overriding reason to react so strongly to Richardson's rather mild comments: The NBA Development League (NBADL) had, since its inception in 2001, rendered the CBA even more fragile and marginal than ever. Yet Coyne and the other CBA bigwigs were still catering to the NBA, just in case the ever-expanding NBADL would be looking for any operation-ready franchises.

In any event, Richardson had apologized to the hecklers immediately after the game and offered another blanket apology to anyone else who might have been offended by his other remarks. "I am not anti-Semitic," he said. "I was giving compliments. It's like saying the NBA is 85 percent black."

After suspending Richardson, the Patroons were quick to issue a public apology. Ben Fernandez, the owner of the franchise and the chairman of the CBA's board of directors, righteously affirmed that the league would not tolerate bigots.

Then, a mere five days after Richardson's suspension, Jim Coyne announced that Micheal Ray's contract with the Patroons would not be renewed. In addition, he would not be allowed to coach Albany's entrée in the upcoming U.S. Basketball League summer season. In so doing, Coyne also claimed that Richardson's alleged anti-Semitic comments were not the only reason for his dismissal. Coyne stated that "prior to all this hoopla," he and Fernandez had discovered that, even though Richardson was under contract to the Patroons, he "had been negotiating with other teams. We pretty much agreed early on he wouldn't be coming back to the CBA."

Richardson's response was to hire a lawyer, John Aretakis, who said that the Patroons actions had put his client's entire coaching career in jeopardy. "Now he would be labeled for the rest of his life as being anti-Semitic, and he's not," said Aretakis. "He's got two kids who are being raised Jewish. He's got an ex-wife he has a good relationship with who is Jewish."

Aretakis was planning to file a law suit against the Hearst Corporation and *Times-Union* sportswriter Brian Ettkin, claiming defamation and slander. In addition to refuting the anti-Semitic accusations, Aretakis said that Richardson's epithet to the hecklers, while a poor choice of words, was commonly used by many men who, like his client, were not homophobic.

The newspaper's managing editor, Mary Fran Gleason, declined to comment.

The Wild, Wild West

Two months after Richardson's dismissal from the Patroons, the CBA board of directors officially cleared him of any wrongdoing, and he quickly landed a job coaching another CBA team—the Oklahoma Cavalry.

Operating as the Oklahoma City Cavalry, the previous incarnation of the franchise had been an expansion team in 1990 when, coached by Charley Rosen, they finished with a league-worst record of 18-38. Replaced by Henry Bibby, the team gradually earned a degree of respectability—culminating in a CBA championship in 1997.

Back then, however, pro basketball was a tough sell in Oklahoma. The most popular sport was college football with the Oklahoma Sooners garnering the vast majority of attention and support. When football wasn't in season, the Oklahoma University hoopers dominated the headlines. One such headline quoted Billy Tubbs, the longtime basketball coach, as saying that he'd rather have his team lead the country in scoring than have them win an NCAA championship.

Another rival was the incredibly successful Oklahoma City Blazers of the Central Hockey League. In winning eight consecutive division championships (1996–2003), the Blazers routinely led all minor-league franchises in every sport by attracting one million spectators per season.

Against such an array of competitors, the CBA-champion OKC Cavalry folded shortly after the 1996–97 campaign.

Eleven years later, a group of local businessmen decided to reincarnate the OKC Cavalry. Their original plan was to join the far-flung and extremely shaky American Basketball Association and use the Abe Lemons Arena on the campus of Oklahoma City University as their home court. Their game plans fell flat when the university backed out of a previously arranged, albeit tenuous agreement. More importantly, the Oklahoma City fathers had focused their attention and their resources on trying to lure an NBA franchise to the City on the Plains. As a result, the OKC Calvary changed course, renamed their team the Oklahoma Cavalry, and moved operations to Lawton where they contracted to play at the Great Plains Coliseum.

With a population that approached 100,000 and made it the state's fifth-largest city, Lawton was situated eighty-seven miles southwest of Oklahoma City. The mostly treeless landscape was typical of the area—large stretches of wild-grass prairie interrupted by an occasional low rolling hill. The primary source of Lawton's economic and population stability was Fort Sill, an army base just outside the city limits. Even though the job market was abetted by a Goodyear Tire and Rubber plant, Lawton's working force generally struggled to make ends meet. Add the extremely hot, dry climate, and it was not surprising that the city had an unusually high crime rate—771.7 violent crimes per 100,000 people, as compared to a nationwide average of 403.6.

Nevertheless, Richardson would so like living and coaching in Lawton that he bought a house in town and, to this day, maintains his permanent residence there.

Along with their coach, the Oklahoma Cavalry thrived in Lawton. Indeed, the only other local competition in the sports-spectator market was Cameron University, a Division II school that had dropped its highly successful football program several years before for financial reasons. Plus, Cameron's hoopsters had not had a winning season since 2004.

Richardson was looking forward to his return to action, but business-as-usual CBA-style had to be changed. "When I was up in Albany," he said, "I had to do all the work. Do the contracts, go out and get the players, be the coach and the general manager. I really couldn't concentrate on just coaching. So when I got the job in Lawton, the first person I contacted was Otis Birdsong. I knew he knew the game and I knew he was someone I could trust."

Birdsong and Richardson had maintained their friendship since Sugar Ray's banishment from the NBA. When Richardson called him, Birdsong was the president and general manager of the Arkansas Rimrockers and had been instrumental in his team's winning the ABA championship. Although the Rimrockers and the ABA were perpetually on the verge of collapse, Birdsong was reluctant to accept Richardson's offer to fulfill the same two positions in Lawton.

"Quite honestly," said Birdsong, "I thought Micheal was just doing it for the money."

But then Birdsong was present when his former teammate conducted a tryout camp in Dallas. "This man really knows what he's doing," Birdsong said, "and I was relieved to discover this." Subsequently, Birdsong signed up to work with his buddy.

Birdsong's new job description included renting an office, finding and signing players, hiring the dancers and the mascot, selling tickets, and once the season commenced, serving as a parking attendant at home games.

Like Richardson, Birdsong had a serious addiction to the game, that is, a Basketball Jones.

In any event, all the necessary components were assembled and Richardson coached with a manic edge. He prowled the sideline, waving his hands and yelling at the officials after virtually every play. Birdsong tried to calm his buddy: "I said, 'Sugar, you can't do that. You have to pick your spots.' But the thing with Micheal is that it was hard for him to find the right balance."

At each and every level of play, it's the rare referee who will tolerate being criticized from tip to buzzer. However, they will usually shrug off the constant nagging if a coach refrains from cursing and/or making personal insults. Moreover, if "short" coaches are usually permitted to stand and walk about, taller coaches (such as the six-foot-five Richardson) will risk getting T'd no matter what they have to say as soon as they rise from their seats. And woe to the vertically gifted coach who approaches a ref and complains about whatever while towering over him.

Richardson's perpetual carping certainly failed to endear him to the league's refs. He once got tossed a minute and twenty seconds into a game. Many opposing players thought he was certifiable.

Richardson wasn't above getting into raging locker-room arguments with his own players. During an early season game, Richardson screamed at a player for not rotating properly on defense. The player's response was to cuss out Richardson for picking on him. Micheal Ray then proceeded to cut the player at halftime.

Despite Richardson's routine hysteria, the expansionist Oklahoma Cavalry finished the season with a 30-18 record, second best in the Western Conference to the Yakima Sun Kings, the CBA's defending champions. Upsetting Yakima in a best-of-five game series, the Calvary advanced to the finals against the Minot Sky Rockets. Just before the first game of the series, Richardson's team officially changed its name to the Lawton–Fort Sill Cavalry as a way of solidifying their association with their home city, and then won the fifth and deciding game to make Sugar Ray a championship coach.

Being a hero in Lawton, Oklahoma, lacked the glamour of being a hoops icon in New York, but Richardson had achieved a sense of peace, comfort, easy living, and acceptance there that changed his life. In many ways, Oklahoma was still the Wild West—a place where a man's past was forgotten, where even an infamous sinner like Richardson could reinvent himself. Indeed, he had been clean for so long that he no longer kept track.

During the off season he bought the house, substituted in the local school system, and even took a local girl as his latest wife. Wherever his journey might lead him, Richardson decided that he'd always return to Lawton.

However, the financial catastrophe that had threatened the CBA since its inception in 1946 finally overwhelmed the league. The NBA Development League had completed its sixth season, and an increasing number of NBA teams began to form farm-system arrangements with D-League teams; providing these affiliates with money, administrators, coaching staffs, and contracted players who needed seasoning and/or more playing time. In addition, even the most well-established NBA players were frequently sent to the appropriate D-League team to get into shape after recuperating from significant injuries.

Under increasing economic distress, the 2008–9 CBA season was suddenly terminated on February 3. In lieu of the traditional long and expensive playoff situation, the 2009 CBA championship was decided in a best-of-three game series between the two teams with the highest winning percentages—the number-two-seeded Albany Patroons versus the number-one-seeded Lawton–Fort Sill Cavalry. To further reduce costs, the entire series was played in Albany.

The Albany media was quick to remind Richardson of the sins of his past, focusing on his most recent humiliation there. But Richardson turned a deaf ear to these constant jibes. After going through "the drug stuff" and the charges of anti-Semitism, he was "able to not get involved in what people say."

Indeed, his revenge on Jim Coyne and the Patroons was to win his second consecutive CBA championship with a thrilling 109–107 victory in overtime. Richardson's elation as short lived, however, when the CBA ceased operations a few weeks later.

Undaunted, the owners of the Cavalry announced they would join another shaky organization, the Premier Basketball League (PBL).

The PBL began in January 2008 with nine teams all situated in the United States. The following season, the Lawton–Fort Sill Calvary was one of thirteen active teams. After compiling a record of 19-2, Richardson's team was clearly the league's best.

According to a rival coach, "Most of Richardson's players were thugs, many were druggies, and some were both. As for Richardson himself, he was the biggest pussy hound in the league. One time, he benched one of his best players for dating the same stripper that he was dating. Another time, Richardson cut a player for getting pregnant another girl that he was dating."

While NBA coaches and their players dating the same woman never seems to have happened, there is at least one instance where a player was sleeping with one of his coach's daughters.

In any event, Richardson coached the Fort Sill Cavalry into the PBL finals. Their ultimate opponents were the Rochester RazorSharks, and the series quickly degenerated into the kind of madcap doings that often afflicted many minor-league basketball games. The owners, the referees, and the players on both sides understood that should a team lose too many games on their home court, the franchise might be in imminent danger of folding. Also, in many cases, hometown fans simply would not tolerate their heroes losing a playoff game—much less in a championship series.

Game one was played in Rochester, and Richardson loudly protested being repeatedly homered by the refs. After being warned several times, he was finally hit with a technical, which seemed to give the RazorSharks' faithful a reason and a license to begin throwing stuff at Richardson. This occurred with 2.6 seconds left in overtime, the RazorSharks up by 110–106 and poised to increase their lead at the free throw line. When a plastic bottle bounced off the top of his head, Richardson pretended not to notice but one of his players was incensed.

This was Oliver Miller, a six-foot-nine veteran of six teams in seven NBA seasons, whose nickname was "The Big O," not because his skill set resembled the great Oscar Robertson—but because Miller usually tipped the scales at 330 pounds and more. He could score (7.4 points per game) and rebound (5.9), but his playing time was always curtailed by his inability to keep pace with NBA action. Before signing with the Cavalry just before the playoffs, Miller had made the usual rounds—Italy, the Harlem Globetrotters, the CBA, ABA, USBL, and a summer in Puerto Rico's Superior League. He was thirty-one when Richardson recruited him and was well aware that as his age and weight increased his playing days were numbered.

While Miller had always manifested a rather peaceful demeanor on the court, he blew his fuse when Richardson was forced to dodge the barrage from the RazorSharks' fans. After engaging in a loud, profane argument with several fans, Miller climbed into the stands to confront his coach's primary tormentor. Fortunately for all concerned, Miller refrained from making physical contact with the fan. Even so, Miller was not only ejected from the game but also suspended for the remainder of the series.

No surprise that this game was Miller's last as a pro.

Yet Miller's penchant for violence seemed to be amped up by his frustration at spending the rest of his life as a civilian.

In April 2011 he was accused of pistol whipping a man during an altercation at a barbecue cookout in Arnold, Maryland. He was accused of, and pled guilty to, charges of first- and second-degree assault, illegally possessing a handgun, using a handgun in a violent crime, and disorderly conduct. He was sentenced to a year in jail and five subsequent years of probation.

In any event, after Miller was banished, Richardson was hopping mad, and the refs tagged him with his second T and automatic ejection. This was followed by some verbal skirmishing between the Rochester fans and several of the Cavalry players. To prevent the incipient riot, and with memories of the Malice in the Palace still vivid, the refs wisely terminated the game, leaving the RazorSharks victorious in the opening gambit of the best-of-three-games series. However, with their coach back on the bench, the series resumed in Oklahoma, and despite the absence of their best player, the Cavalry won the championship with a pair of blowout victories.

Added to the team's two previous CBA championships, Richardson had now led the Cavalry to three consecutive titles. Even so, not a single NBA team contacted him about being an assistant coach or an advance or a college scout. Nothing. Not even a congratulatory phone call or email.

Richardson's perpetual banishment is even more alarming when considering the case of Kevin Mackey.

After a few years coaching a high-school team in his native Boston, Mackey became an assistant coach at Boston University. In 1983 he made the next step when he was hired to be the head coach at Cleveland State University. His tenure there was hugely successful. Employing a "run 'n stun" game plan, Mackey's teams earned one NCAA and two NIT appearances while averaging more than twenty wins per season. His best team was the 1985–

86 edition, which won a school-record 29 wins and became the first fourteenth seed to advance into the NCAA's Sweet Sixteen.

On the strength of that season, Mackey became a celebrity in northeastern Ohio. With the money earned from that 1986 NCAA run, Cleveland State built a new fieldhouse, and the media took to calling Mackey "the King of Cleveland."

But Mackey's reign proved to be precarious.

A long-time alcoholic, Mackey began snorting cocaine shortly after that glorious season.

Still, Mackey was a rising star, and on July 11, 1990, Cleveland State signed him to a two-year contract worth $300,000 (the equivalent of $541,544 in 2014).

Then, only two days after re-upping with Cleveland State, Mackey—in the company of two crack prostitutes—spent nine hours in a crack house on the corner of Eddy Road and Edmonton Avenue. Meanwhile, acting on a phone tip, the Cleveland police saw his brand-new Lincoln Town Car parked in front of the house. Since there were no reports of the car having been stolen, they staked out the address.

The police continued to track Mackey when he and his two companions left the house and climbed into the car. Their excuse to stop and arrest Mackey came when he repeatedly drove the car into oncoming traffic. A urine sample taken at the police station showed traces of cocaine. Also, Mackey (who claimed he fainted during blood tests) was discovered to have a pair of large needle pokes in his right thigh.

He subsequently pleaded no contest, was ordered to undergo a sixty-day treatment in a rehabilitation center—and was summarily fired by Cleveland State.

For the next several years, Mackey labored in pro basketball's nether world: variously coaching the Miami Tropics, the Portland (Maine) Mountain Cats, and the Atlantic City Seagulls in the summertime USBL. There never was any doubt that Mackey was an exceptional coach—he was the only USBL coach to win three consecutive championships. Add still another title when Mackey led the Mansfield Hawks to the championship of the International Basketball Association.

Then, in 2004 Mackey was hired as a scout by Larry Bird, the president of basketball operations for the Indiana Pacers. Turned out that the early years of Bird's active career with the Boston Celtics coincided with Mackey's tenure at Boston College. Mackey was still with the Pacers during the 2013–14 season.

So not only was Mackey welcomed into the NBA but has become a fixture on Indiana's scouting staff. While Micheal Richardson is still banned from the league.

Perhaps it's merely a coincidence that Mackey is white and Richardson is a black man.

Perhaps not.

18

The Most Shameful Playoff Series in the History of Professional Basketball

Under Richardson's guidance, the Lawton–Fort Sill Cavalry finished the Premier Basketball League's 2010–11 regular season at 17-2. After surviving the preliminary playoff series, the Cavalry squared off for a rematch with the Rochester RazorSharks in the best-of-three-game finals.

On April 15 Rochester won the first game at home, and the Cavalry evened the series back in Oklahoma—setting up a do-or-die final contest, also in Oklahoma. But there were several reasons why the Cavalry never really had a chance to repeat as champs.

That's because the owner of the RazorSharks, a Chicago podiatrist named Sev Hrywnak, was also the commissioner of the PBL. The long-honored tradition in minor-league basketball was to have only local refs work playoff games. However, even though most of the RazorSharks' playoff road games were presided over by the same pair of Rochester born-and-raised refs, Hrywnak claimed he had nothing to do with assigning the officials. According to Hrywnak, the assignments were purely accidental. However, in a previous semifinal victory by the RazorSharks in Quebec, the hometown fans were provoked into a near riot when the Rochester refs awarded the visitors seventy-one free throws.

After Rochester eliminated Quebec, the losing coach, Rob Spon, reported that the third official in the last game—the only one not from Rochester—told him, "I've never been involved in anything like this."

Similar complaints came from every team that Rochester bested on their way to the championship series. The general manager of the Halifax Rainmen, Ian McCarthy, thought that in their first-round series, the profound bias of the Rochester refs was "blatantly obvious."

The numbers in the PBL finals certainly supported the general allegations of game fixing: In the second halves of the final two games, the Cavalry shot a total of three free throws. In the entire three-game championship series the RazorSharks outshot the Cavalry from the stripe by 104–49.

Why, then, were the Cavalry "allowed" to win the second game of the series? Most likely to insure another payday for both teams.

In any event, during the third and deciding contest, the Cavalry's play-by-play radio announcer opined on the air that the imported refs, led by a "belligerent, black-haired official . . . *are* under orders to steal this game."

Despite some incredibly perverse calls by one of the Rochester refs and an overwhelming edge in free throws attempted by the RazorSharks, the Cavalry netted a steady barrage of treys from beyond the arc and were down by only a single point late in the fourth quarter. Then came a play that irrevocably turned the game.

One of the Cavalry's guards drove into the lane and collided with a Rochester player who clearly arrived at the point of impact late. The nearest ref was the only local one, and he quickly and decisively made the correct call: a block. But the black-haired ref raced over from the far side of the court and changed the call to a charge.

"When I seen that," Richardson said later, "I wanted to run out there and kill him."

Which is precisely what Richardson attempted to do shortly thereafter.

With 0.6 seconds left in the game, Rochester had the ball and a three-point lead, so to save themselves from the fans' angry threats, the refs dashed off the court and headed for their locker room. Micheal Ray ran after them, darting underneath the bleachers, pushing his way through the irate crowd and the intervening police. Fortunately for all concerned, the refs reached their sanctuary and locked the door just before Richardson got there.

The day after the game, Richardson was still hot. The game and the entire series, he said, was a "disgrace to professional sports."

Hrywnak responded with venom to Richardson's reactions: "From what I was told by other coaches and fans, during the season he got away with more than any other coach." Hrywnak on to say that "the people in Albany" told him not to allow Richardson in his league. "The guy got a second and a third chance, and he blew it."

Hrywnak also announced that the head of the PBL's officials had resigned because of the "false accusations" that had been made. Moreover, he said he was initiating legal action against the Cavalry's radio announcer and would do the same against anybody else who charged that the games were fixed.

On April 19, 2011, the Cavalry along with every other PBL team (with the lone exception of Rochester) severed their respective connections with Hrywnak's organization.

The next day, the owners of Lawton–Fort Sill franchise announced that financial considerations forced them to suspend operations entirely.

Epilogue   *Whither Sugar Ray?*

A score of professional athletes were allowed to resume their careers despite having committed worse transgressions than Richardson has.

On July 1, 2009, J. R. Smith was driving through a thirty-five-miles-per-hour stretch of highway near Millstone, New Jersey, and was officially clocked at sixty-seven miles per hour, when he blew a stop sign and collided with another vehicle. Smith suffered only a few minor scratches; the two passengers in the other car were hospitalized with severe injuries but survived. The most tragic result of the accident was the death of Andre Bell, a lifelong buddy of Smith, who was sitting alongside him.

Although Smith had been issued four previous speeding tickets, and had twenty-eight points on his license, a grand jury declined to issue an indictment of vehicular homicide. But Smith didn't escape his just deserts. He was sentenced to ninety days in jail, yet served only twenty-four days.

Three years later (May 24, 2012), Smith was arrested once more for failing to appear in a Miami Beach court as a consequence of his having been charged with operating a motor scooter without a license. This time, Smith was released on bond after spending just a few hours in a jail cell.

Neither of these incidents moved the NBA to either ban or suspend Smith from playing.

Likewise has the NFL ignored the criminality of several players: Like Josh Brent, a defensive end for the Dallas Cowboys, who was convicted of intoxicated manslaughter in January 2014. Accordingly, Brent was fined $10,000, was sentenced to 180 days behind bars, 45 days in a rehabilitation center, and placed on probation for ten years.

On November 25, 2014, slightly ten months after his conviction, and after serving a ten-game suspension imposed by the Cowboys, Brent took the field against the New York Giants. Plus, Dallas subsequently signed Brent to a nonguaranteed contract for the 2015 season.

Then there's the infamous case of Michael Vick, imprisoned for twenty-one months for running a dog-fighting operation. After his release his career resumed with the Philadelphia Eagles and the New York Jets.

(In addition, from January 1, 2010, to September 1, 2014, the arrest rates of NFL, NBA, and MLB are substantial. Calculated as the number of arrests per year as per a U.S. population of 100,000, the NFL's number is 2,446, the NBA's is 2,151, and MLB's is 553—virtually all of these for domestic assault or DUI. Nationally, the rate per 100,000 population for assault arrests is 241 and for DUI is 809.)

In any event, that's at least three jailbirds whose careers (and bank accounts) were resurrected. Among NBA miscreants, players officially forgiven for either domestic assault and/or DUI arrests include the likes of Jason Kidd, Kendrick Perkins (twice), Greg Oden, Ty Lawson, Kyle Lowry, and many more.

Meanwhile, Richardson never spent any time behind bars and never harmed anybody except himself. Nor has he ever identified any of the "all-stars" he often shared a pipe with. "I don't want to get into naming names," he says. "For whatever reasons, they didn't get caught and I did. It's about how I fucked up, not them."

Why, then, has no NBA team offered Richardson a job as scout or assistant coach? "I have no idea," says Richardson. "I do know that if David Stern wanted to, he could have done something for me."

Perhaps Richardson is being blackballed simply because he's the first and perpetual example of what will happen if an NBA player accumulates three strikes. "But, hey," he shrugs, "who says that life should be fair?"

For sure, Micheal Ray Richardson swears that he's a happy man—and, on some level, he assuredly is. "I do some substitute teaching in the Lawton schools," he says, "and Otis Birdsong and I do nine weeks of summer camps for kids in Palm Beach. I get my NBA pension, and I made some good money playing for thirteen years overseas. Am I rich? No. But I'm doing okay."

Despite winning championships in three different leagues, however, Micheal Ray has had his fill of coaching in the minors. "I've got nothing more to prove at that level," he says.

He's also moved on from the anger, guilt, and shame that shadowed his life for so long. "Yes, I brought all of that shit on myself, but I've paid my dues. All I ask is that people don't judge me for what I did over thirty-five years ago."

Even David Stern believes that Richardson has paid his dues. Stern was always plagued by a modicum of guilt for having had to ban Richardson from the NBA. When Stern finally retired as the league's commissioner in 2015, he was nevertheless instrumental in welcoming Micheal Ray back into the league's good graces. Beginning in November 2016, Richardson was hired by the NBA to conduct basketball camps for youths in India, Indonesia, and Africa.

However, if Micheal Ray Richardson's sins have been officially redeemed, the NBA is still suffering from its own self-created problems.

Indeed, the self-indulgence of too many modern-day players, and the increasing emphasis on flash over substance by both the league and the media, has done much to reduce the NBA to just another "product." There's no doubt that the overall glamorization-cum-commercialization of The Game is much more criminal than anything Micheal Ray Richardson has ever done.

A Note on Sources

All quotes accompanied by present-day citations—"he says," "he recalls," and so forth—come from personal interviews. Thanks, then, to Micheal Ray Richardson, Darryl Dawkins, Derrick Rowland, Ross Barrett, Steve Patterson, Pace Manion, Phil Jackson, Jim Cleamons, Hubie Brown, Tom Nissalke, Fred Kerber, Calvin Ramsey, Earl Monroe, Tim Layden, Tim Wilkins, Frankie Sanders, Eric Musselman, and Neal Walk. Various online quotes from Micheal Ray Richardson were used from articles on Jud Heathcote and Jim Brandenburg. I also used various online articles, which include *NewsOne*, "72 Percent of Black Kids Raised by Single Parent, 25% Overall in U.S."; and *Psychology Today*, "Father Absence, Father Deficit, Father Hunger," May 23, 2012. Print sources used include Brian Tuohy's *Larceny Games*, David Leonard's *After Artest*, Jim Patton's *Il Basket d'Italia*, Neil D. Isaacs's *Vintage NBA*, as well as my own titles *The Wizard of Odds*, *The Scandals of '51*, and *Perfectly Awful*.